P9-DGL-860

YANKEE DOODLE
GALS

**WOMEN PILOTS
OF WORLD WAR II**

BY AMY NATHAN

FOREWORD BY NASA ASTRONAUT
EILEEN COLLINS

NATIONAL GEOGRAPHIC SOCIETY
WASHINGTON, D.C.

**Dedicated to the WASPs and the WAFS—
and to the memory of my mother and father,
who were also members of that great generation.**

Copyright © 2001 Amy Nathan

All rights reserved. Reproduction of the whole or any part of the contents without written permission from the National Geographic Society is strictly prohibited.

Book Design by Gerry Greaney, Greaney Design

Text is set in Minion; display type is in Eagle Bold, House Broken Clean, and Trade Gothic Bold Condensed

Library of Congress Cataloging-in-Publication Data
Nathan, Amy.
Yankee doodle gals : women pilots of World War II /
by Amy Nathan ; with a foreword by Eileen Collins.
p.   cm.
ISBN 0-7922-8216-7 (Hardcover)

1. Women Airforce Service Pilots (U.S.)—Juvenile literature. 2. Women air pilots—United States—Juvenile literature. 3. Air pilots, Military—United States—Juvenile literature. 4. World War, 1939–1945—Aerial operations, American—Juvenile literature. 5. World War, 1939–1945—Participation, Female—Juvenile literature. [1. Women Airforce Service Pilots (U.S.). 2. Women air pilots. 3. World War, 1939–1945—Participation, Female.] I. Title.
D790 .N38 2001
940.54'4973'082—dc21
2001000560

The world's largest nonprofit scientific and educational organization, the National Geographic Society was founded in 1888 "for the increase and diffusion of geographic knowledge." Since then it has supported scientific exploration and spread information to its more than eight million members worldwide. The National Geographic Society educates and inspires millions every day through magazines, books, television programs, videos, maps and atlases, research grants, the National Geographic Bee, teacher workshops, and innovative classroom materials. The Society is supported through membership dues, charitable gifts, and income from the sale of its educational products. Members receive NATIONAL GEOGRAPHIC magazine— the Society's official journal—discounts on Society products and other benefits. For more information about the National Geographic Society, its educational programs and publications, and ways to support its work, please call 1-800 NGS-LINE (647-5463) or write to the following address:

National Geographic Society
1145 17th Street N.W.
Washington, D.C. 20036-4688
U.S.A.

Visit the Society's Web site: www.nationalgeographic.com

Printed in the United States of America

Published by the National Geographic Society

John M. Fahey, Jr., President and Chief Executive Officer

Gilbert M. Grosvenor, Chairman of the Board

Nina D. Hoffman, Executive Vice President, President of Books and School Publishing

Staff for this book

Nancy Laties Feresten, Vice President, Editor-in-Chief, Children's Books

Bea Jackson, Art Director, Children's Books

Suzanne Patrick Fonda, Project Editor

Carl Mehler, Director of Maps

Matt Chwastyk and Greg Ugiansky, Map Research and Production

Meredith C. Wilcox, Illustrations Assistant

Jo H. Tunstall, Assistant Editor

Deborah E. Patton, Indexer

Lewis R. Bassford, Production Manager

Vincent P. Ryan, Manufacturing Manager

Photo Credits

Front and back covers, 15, 18 lo, 19, 21 (both), 24 lo, 28, 30 (both), 32, 33 up, 36, 42 up, 44–45, 47 up, 52 rt, 53, 60 up, 62, 63 le, 66, 68, 69, 74, 77, 81 courtesy National Archives; title pages, 37, 38 (both), 39, 40, 41, 42 lo, 46, 47 lo le, 47 lo rt, 48, 50 lo, 52 le, 56, 57, 58, 63 rt, 70–71, 84 courtesy the Woman's Collection, Texas Woman's University; p. 4 courtesy NASA; pp. 6, 16, 18 up, 31, 33 lo, 50 up, 51, 60 lo, 73 Courtesy United States Air Force Museum; pp. 9 up, 55, 78 courtesy Barbara Erickson London; p. 9 lo copyright © Disney Enterprises, Inc.; pp. 10, 26 courtesy Gene Shaffer Fitzpatrick; p. 11 courtesy Dora Dougherty Strother; p. 13 up courtesy Museum of Flight, Seattle; p. 13 lo courtesy Teresa James; pp. 14, 64 courtesy Betty Jane Williams; p. 20 courtesy Air Force Historical Research Agency, Maxwell AFB; p. 22 courtesy Florene Miller Watson; p. 24 up courtesy the Gillies family; pp. 25, 34–35 Peter Stackpole/Time Pix; pp. 27 up, 79 courtesy Maggie Gee; pp. 27 lo (SI Neg. No. 79-13664), 72 up (SI Neg. No. A-45978) Courtesy National Air and Space Museum, Smithsonian Institution; p. 54 courtesy Margaret Ray Ringenberg; pp. 65, 76 courtesy Library of Congress; p. 72 lo courtesy United States Air Force Museum, Hugh Morgan photographer; p. 82 courtesy United States Air Force Academy, Elissa Arnesen photographer; p. 85 le U.S. Air Force photo courtesy Kimberly Olson; p. 85 rt courtesy M'Lis Ward; p. 86 U.S. Navy photo, Lt. jg Andrea Kowal photographer.

FRONT AND BACK COVERS:
JANE STRAUGHAN, A FERRY PILOT, GRADUATED FROM THE FIRST CLASS TO COMPLETE JACKIE COCHRAN'S TRAINING PROGRAM.

TITLE PAGE:
ONE WASP PILOT WATCHES AS ANOTHER FLIES BY, PULLING A CLOTH TARGET TO BE SHOT AT BY GUNNERS ON THE GROUND.

IN 1995, EILEEN COLLINS
BECAME THE FIRST WOMAN
TO PILOT A SPACE SHUTTLE
AND, IN 1999, THE FIRST
WOMAN COMMANDER OF A
SPACE SHUTTLE MISSION.
WOMEN FIRST BECAME NASA
ASTRONAUTS IN 1978.
BY THE YEAR 2000, 35 OF
NASA'S 154 ASTRONAUTS
WERE WOMEN.

FOREWORD

By Eileen Collins,
Colonel, U.S. Air Force, NASA Astronaut

I first learned about the WASPs when I was in college in the early 1970s. I'd been interested in flying for several years and had read numerous books on aviation. Most of the books were about male pilots, as it was still unusual for women to fly. There were only a few female airline pilots then. There were no female pilots at all in the U.S. Air Force. I figured that's how it had always been—until I found a book about Jackie Cochran and discovered that for two years during World War II, more than a thousand women flew military aircraft: fighters, bombers, trainers, and transports. They were the WASPs. Pilots Jackie Cochran and Nancy Love were their leaders.

It was then that I decided: This is something I want to do!

I soon got my chance. In 1976, the Air Force started admitting a small number of women into active-duty pilot training. Two years later, during my last year at Syracuse University, I applied for Air Force pilot training and was one of the few women lucky enough to be accepted. It had been more than 30 years since the WASP program ended. At last women were flying military aircraft again. It helped to know about the WASPs, to know that women had already done this, that it wasn't impossible. Their love of flying gave them the courage to try something society didn't really expect women to do: take to the skies. Their courage inspired me to follow my dreams, too.

In 1990, I was selected by NASA to become an astronaut. I remembered the WASPs and felt a great responsibility to do a good job so there would be more opportunities for women in the future. In 1995, on my first flight as pilot of the space shuttle, I thought I had better not make a mistake because I wanted to set a good precedent for other women, just as the WASPs had done.

Although the WASP program was short-lived, the outstanding performance of these pilots helped open up opportunities for women in my generation and in generations to come. WASPs trained hard, took risks, did a great job, and served their country. They also got to do something they loved to do: fly!

WITH A PICTURE OF FIFI, THEIR MASCOT, ON THEIR JACKETS, THESE WASPS FLEW B-17 BOMBERS, LIKE THE ONE SHOWN HERE, NAMED "PISTOL PACKIN' MAMA" IN HONOR OF THE WASPS.

1

THE CHANCE
OF A LIFETIME

A small, battered plane zoomed over the sizzling California desert. Bullets whizzed by the cockpit, as soldiers down on the sand shot off round after round of gunfire. Luckily, no bullets hit that little plane. The gutsy young woman in the pilot's seat made another safe landing. She was also helping to make history. It was early in 1944, during World War II. The pilot, Nonie Horton Anderson, belonged to a special group of women pilots—the WASPs (Women Airforce Service Pilots). They made history by being the first women trained to fly military planes on a whole range of missions for the U.S. armed forces.

EAGER TO HELP

"That was the most fun I had in my life," remembers Nonie (a nickname for Leonora). "It was beautiful flying back and forth over the desert." The troops doing the shooting weren't the enemy. They were young American soldiers. WASPs gave these young men practice aiming at moving targets in the sky so the soldiers would be ready to fight real battles overseas. The soldiers didn't actually shoot at a WASP's plane. They aimed at a long piece of cloth that trailed along behind the plane, attached by a strong cable. Sometimes inexperienced soldiers shot a WASP's plane by mistake. They never hit Nonie's plane, but she says a classmate's plane was hit. The gunners used real ammunition. Was it dangerous? "You don't think of those things," says Nonie. She had a job to do, and she did it.

Nonie felt lucky to be flying at all. Before World War II, the U.S. military wouldn't use women as pilots. Neither would the airlines. Most people still thought flying was a "man's job." It was hard for a woman pilot to find a flying job. Airplanes had been around for only a few dozen years. Most Americans had never been in a plane. Not many people had learned to be pilots, especially not many women.

But nearly 3,000 American women had managed to learn to fly by the time the United States entered World War II at the end of 1941. They wanted to use their flying skills to help their country. They had a tough time persuading the Army to give them a chance. The Army handled most military flying back then. (The U.S. Air Force as a separate branch of the military wasn't created until after the war.)

Finally, in late 1942, the Army created two new groups just for women pilots—groups that a year later combined to become the WASPs.

The 1,102 women who served in these new units weren't allowed to fly overseas, where all World War II battles took place. They flew mainly in the United States, doing military flying that didn't involve combat. Men who would otherwise do those jobs could then go overseas to the battlefronts.

FLY GIRLS

At first, Army officials worried about the skills of these "fly girls," as some people called them. (Male pilots were called "fly boys.") But WASPs proved that women could fly as well as men, and as safely, too. WASPs flew every kind of plane the Army had. "We were able to fly all these marvelous airplanes. This was probably the greatest experience in our lives for all of us," notes Barbara Erickson London.

Their expert flying skills earned them another nickname: "hot pilot" (slang for a super flier). Some WASPs jokingly called themselves "Miss H.P." However, many missions were risky, even for a tough H.P. Thirty-eight of these women pilots died flying for their country.

"Our country was in danger then. There was great pride in doing your part," says Florene Miller Watson. The United States entered the war after Japanese planes bombed American airfields and ships at Pearl Harbor, in Hawaii, in December 1941. Both Japan and its ally, Nazi Germany, were launching attacks on many countries. The United States believed it had to try to put a stop to that.

WASP Maggie Gee notes, "I felt I had an obligation to do something to help." B.J. (Betty Jane) Williams adds, "When you can do your part and do something you love, it's terrific!"

However, the WASPs' final challenge was the toughest of all. As the war started going better for the United States, the armed forces didn't need so many pilots. The Army decided to end the WASP program in December 1944, several months before the war was over. It would be about 30 years before American women had a chance to fly for the military again.

This book tells the story of Nonie, Florene, B.J., Barbara, Maggie, and the more than one thousand other young women who served in the WASPs. Some had just finished high school or were in college when they joined. Others were teachers, nurses, models, writers, engineers, librarians, flight instructors, or office workers. They gladly stopped what they had been doing for the chance of a lifetime—the chance to fly fantastic planes for their country. Although their mission was cut short, they helped open the skies for women, proving that a woman's place can very well be inside a cockpit.

BARBARA ERICKSON LONDON (ABOVE, LEFT) IN A P-51 MUSTANG FIGHTER PLANE, WITH FELLOW PILOT EVELYN SHARP. EVELYN WAS ONE OF THE 38 WOMEN PILOTS WHO DIED WHILE FLYING FOR THEIR COUNTRY. SHE WAS KILLED WHEN THE ENGINE FAILED IN A NEW PLANE SHE WAS DELIVERING FOR THE ARMY.

FIFI
THE WASP MASCOT

CLOSE-UP

WASPs had a cartoon mascot named Fifi, a winged creature with goggles and leather boots designed by artists at Walt Disney Studios. Most U.S. military units in World War II had cartoon mascots, which decorated everything from jackets to bombers.

Fifi came from *The Gremlins,* a children's book written in 1942 by Roald Dahl. At the time, he was a young British pilot. His book told of imaginary creatures that played tricks on pilots. He named male mischiefmakers "gremlins"; a female one was a "fifinella," or "fifi."

WASPs felt Fifi wasn't as naughty as a male gremlin. "She kept the sand out of your gas tank and kept the engine running," Nonie Horton Anderson explains. B.J. Williams adds, "Fifi helped us come home safely."

GENE SHAFFER FITZPATRICK, AGE 17 (LEFT), INTERVIEWING
AMELIA EARHART (CENTER) FOR THE HIGH SCHOOL PAPER

2 FLYING FEVER

"Since I was seven years old, I've been interested in flying," remembers Gene Shaffer Fitzpatrick, another WASP. "It looked kind of spectacular. I can remember walking to grammar school in the mornings, and there was this airplane that went right over our path. It was a small plane. I'd see that and I'd go, 'Someday I'm going to be doing that.'"

FLYING DREAMS

Like Gene, many WASPs grew up during the 1920s and 1930s and fell in love with flying as young girls. "I grew up at the time when aviation was just beginning," explains Maggie Gee. "Flying was an exciting thing to do. Today maybe kids would want to go to the moon and be astronauts. Back then, the exciting thing was to be a pilot."

"Our heroes back then weren't movie stars and rock stars. Our heroes were the people who were pushing back the frontiers in the sky, people who had made headlines, gone faster, gone farther," notes Dora Dougherty Strother.

Airplanes were so new that many families would visit nearby airports on weekends just to look at these flying machines. "We'd watch the planes take off. It was a Sunday thing to do," recalls Maggie. On one airport visit, seven-year-old Gene saw Charles Lindbergh, the famous pilot who in 1927 was the first person to fly solo, nonstop across the Atlantic Ocean. A few months after this flight, he came to Gene's hometown airport in California to fly in an air race. Gene watched him climb into his plane and zoom off.

Later, Gene met another top pilot: Amelia Earhart. In 1932, she was the first woman to fly solo, nonstop across the Atlantic. In 1937, she disappeared forever during an around-the-world flight. Just before that flight, she came to Gene's local airport. Gene, who was 17 at the time, went there to interview this famous flier for the school paper. "Amelia was so nice," Gene recalls. "She didn't talk down to me. She said, 'Gee, kid, if you want to fly, go do it.'"

DORA DOUGHERTY STROTHER (FAR RIGHT IN PHOTO) WITH HER MOTHER AND BROTHERS ON AN AIRPORT VISIT

Gene's dream of flying surprised her parents. "My mother was against it," Gene reports. "She said it wasn't ladylike." In those days, most people felt flying was just for men. That didn't stop Gene.

"It takes a certain type of person to go off and do something different, like being a pilot," Maggie notes. What gave Maggie and Gene the courage to do that? Maggie says that as a little girl she "liked to do things that were a little different. I liked science, and I played ball with the boys. Girls didn't do that so much then." Gene points out that she was more adventurous than her sisters, more interested in the outdoors. She also kept

her dream of flying alive "by reading every book in the library on flying."

Dora thanks her mom, who stressed the importance of learning and "was supportive of anything I might want to do. I never had a feeling I was different from my brothers in what I could do," notes Dora, who liked building model airplanes with her brothers. Faith Buchner Richards also feels her independent spirit came from her mom. "My mother was a college professor. In those days, not many women did that either," Faith explains. "I never thought there were any limits to what a woman could do."

UP WITH BARNSTORMERS

Some WASPs not only dreamed about planes as girls, they flew in them. "That was kind of unusual in those days," remarks Florene Miller Watson. "I was about eight years old when I took my first airplane ride. I went flying with barnstormers." These were daring pilots who traveled around the country in small planes during the 1920s and 1930s, putting on air shows, performing amazing stunts, and selling tickets to give people rides.

"The barnstormers would come flying over town and burp their throttles: *whirp, whirp, whirp*," remembers Florene, who grew up in a small town in northern Texas. "When we heard that noise, everybody would run outside to see an airplane up there. He'd land out in the prairie somewhere." People rushed out to find the plane.

"My father would buy me a ticket and let me ride," Florene recalls. Barnstormers' planes had cockpits that were open to the air. "I'd sit in that cockpit with the wind blowing my hair and peek over the side. In those

days, you didn't know what the ground would look like from a bird's-eye view. We didn't have television or many photographs of what the world looked like from the air. It was a whole new world for me. I thought I was a bird! I liked it from the start."

Dora also took a ride in a small plane as a girl. "When I was about 12 years old, my father treated my family to an airplane ride. The flight was short, and the plane was just big enough for five passengers. When the plane climbed over the airport, I felt as if I were floating. I felt like Alice in Wonderland. Here was a big, wonderful, exciting new world. I knew then that I wanted to be a part of that world."

Not all WASPs caught flying fever as little girls. Nonie Horton Anderson was in college when the flying bug bit her. A friend gave her a ride in his small plane. "I liked to take photos from the air," Nonie reports. "I was crazy about it."

IN THE 1920s, BARNSTORMERS PERFORMED WILD STUNTS, SUCH AS THIS UPSIDE-DOWN ATTEMPT TO GRAB A HAT. IN 1938, A LAW PUT AN END TO SUCH DANGEROUS TRICKS.

FLYING LESSONS

Becoming a pilot was hard, not just because people thought it wasn't ladylike. Flying lessons were expensive. During the 1930s, the United States went through a tough time called the Great Depression. It was hard enough for people to afford the basics. Paying for extras like flying lessons was out of the question for most families. Taking enough lessons to earn a beginner's pilot's license could cost more than $500, equal to about four months' pay for a typical factory worker back then.

Only a few future WASPs came from families wealthy enough to afford these lessons easily. Sara Chapin Winston's well-to-do family lived in a Michigan suburb. She earned her pilot's license on her 16th birthday. Even so, she did odd jobs at her local airport, such as cutting the grass, to earn extra money so she could rent an airplane to practice with after she had her license.

Florene's dad owned jewelry stores and could afford to buy his own plane. "My father was afraid America was going to get into the war," she explains. "He wanted his children to be able to contribute to the war effort by knowing how to fly." So in 1940, 20-year-old Florene took time off from Baylor University to come home and take flying lessons in her dad's new plane.

TERESA JAMES WAS ONE OF THE FEW WOMEN BARNSTORMERS.

13

But for most people, paying for flying lessons wasn't easy. In 1939, the government decided to help. War seemed likely to break out in Europe. If the United States became involved, it would need more pilots. So the Army set up low-cost classes—Civilian Pilot Training (CPT) classes—which were offered mainly at colleges. For only $40, students could learn to fly in these classes. At first, about one woman was admitted for every ten men. Barbara Erickson London took these classes in 1940 while she was in college at the University of Washington, in Seattle.

Unfortunately, this great deal soon ended for women. In June 1941, the Army decided it could afford to train only people who might someday fly in combat, something it didn't plan to let women do. Women weren't allowed to take CPT classes anymore. But by then, these classes had already turned hundreds of young women into pilots, including Barbara, Dora, and Faith. Barbara even won a flying competition in Seattle, beating all other CPT students, male and female. After that, she became a CPT teacher herself. Dora recalls how she felt the first time she flew a plane all by herself during the CPT classes she took at Northwestern University, in Illinois: "I felt I might explode with excitement. But most of all, I felt proud. I could fly as well as the boys. I could be a pilot!"

Taking flying lessons was much harder for women who missed out on the CPT classes and whose families weren't wealthy. After high school, Gene worked in an office. By 1941, at age 21, she was finally earning enough to spare some cash for lessons at a nearby airport. The cost: $6 for a half-hour lesson, about one-third of her weekly pay. For a basic license—a "private" license—she had to take enough lessons to prove she had flown for 35 hours.

Then bad luck struck. After Gene took a few lessons, her California airport suddenly closed in December 1941. That's when Japan surprised the world by attacking Pearl Harbor in Hawaii, causing the United States to enter World War II. After that, the government stopped all nonmilitary flying at airports near the coasts so the armed forces could keep a close watch on all planes coming to the United States. That would make it harder for an enemy plane to sneak in and attack. Gene didn't give up. She borrowed money from a friend's dad and moved to Nevada for a few months to take flying lessons at an airport that was open because it wasn't near the coast.

Nonie had the same problem. While working as a schoolteacher in Washington, D.C., she drove on weekends to a New Jersey airport for flying lessons. When that airport closed in 1941 because it was too near the East Coast, she drove farther inland to take lessons in Pennsylvania.

B.J. WILLIAMS

14

CLOSE-UP

CORNELIA FORT

BOMBS IN THE SKY

After Cornelia Fort finished Sarah Lawrence College in 1940, she wanted a new challenge. She tried a flying lesson, loved it, and quickly earned her pilot's license, surprising her wealthy Tennessee family. In 1941, 23-year-old Cornelia headed for Hawaii to teach flying there.

She flew with her students in small training planes over Pearl Harbor, a busy Hawaiian port filled with U.S. ships. She and a student were in such a plane on the morning of December 7, 1941—the day Japan launched its surprise air attack on Pearl Harbor.

That morning, a plane zoomed right at her—a Japanese plane. She pulled up on her controls to keep from being hit. "I looked quickly at Pearl Harbor and my spine tingled when I saw billowing black smoke," she wrote later in a magazine article. "I looked way up and saw the formations of silver bombers. . . . Something detached itself from an airplane and came glistening down. My eyes followed it down, down and . . . my heart turned . . . when the bomb exploded in the middle of the harbor. I knew the air was not the place for my little baby airplane and I set about landing as quickly as ever I could."

She and her student escaped safely. The next year, Cornelia was one of the first to join the new women's pilot group that later became known as the WASPs.

JITTERS

"My gosh, aren't you scared out of your wits? Aren't you afraid to be up there by yourself?" That's what Florene's friends asked her. She didn't have a bad case of the jitters when she started flying, but some of the women did. As a teen, Teresa James was terrified of flying but took lessons anyway, to impress a boy she was dating. After a few lessons, she was hooked, and her jitters disappeared; soon she forgot about that guy. By age 21, she had become a barnstormer, thrilling crowds with stunts like making 26 spinning turns in midair.

Some parents, like Gene's mom, were nervous about letting their daughters fly. But other parents, like Barbara's mom, were supportive. "If that was what I wanted to do, she would let me do it," reports Barbara.

"You only fear what you don't understand," explains B.J. Williams, who learned to fly in CPT classes. "When you learn to fly, you're taught the theory of flight and why the plane doesn't fall like a brick. Fear never entered the picture for me. The moment I was in a plane and the instructor turned the controls over to me on the first ride, I knew this was what I wanted to do."

These young women loved the independence, the excitement, and the beauty of soaring through the air. "Anybody that hasn't seen the world from up there hasn't really seen it," reports Barbara. "It's a beautiful sight, flying up there between the clouds. It kind of puts you in your place as to how big you think you really are."

JACKIE COCHRAN,
WITH A P-51 MUSTANG

BIRTH OF THE WASPS

Those independent-minded young women who loved whizzing through the sky wanted to use their skills to help their country. They had their chance, thanks to the two talented women pilots who would become the leaders of the WASPs: Jacqueline "Jackie" Cochran and Nancy Love. It took a long time, a lot of hard work, and a bit of luck for these two women to persuade the Army to give female fliers a try. Having lunch with the President helped, too.

JACKIE'S LETTER

Jackie Cochran was one of the most famous women pilots of the 1940s. It wasn't just her fame that made people pay attention to her. "Jackie had the kind of personality that you didn't say no to her. She'd figure out a way to get what she wanted," remembers B.J. Williams. Jackie's toughness helped her survive a rough childhood as an orphan, living in small southern towns. Her foster family was so poor that she said she had to quit elementary school to go to work in a cotton mill. But Jackie was determined to make something of herself. By her mid-20s, she had moved to New York City. She worked at a fancy beauty salon there, dreaming of starting a cosmetics company. At a party, she met a millionaire businessman (whom she later married). He recommended that she become a pilot so she could fly around the country selling cosmetics. So Jackie took flying lessons and earned her license in just three weeks.

She eventually started her own cosmetics company, but flying won her heart. She started winning air races and earned an award for being the best female flier of the year in 1937, just five years after learning to fly. Jackie wrote in her book *The Stars at Noon*, "I might have been born in a hovel, but I determined to travel with the wind and the stars."

Soon more than air races were on her mind. Hitler's German Army invaded Poland in September 1939, causing Britain and France to declare war to try to stop Hitler's Nazis from taking over Europe. World War II had started. The United States wasn't in the war yet, but Americans worried that their soldiers soon might have to fight, too. Shortly after Germany took over Poland, Jackie wrote to Eleanor Roosevelt, the President's wife.

JACKIE WITH GENERAL HAP ARNOLD,
HEAD OF THE ARMY AIR FORCES

Mrs. Roosevelt was a supporter of women's rights. She had even taken a few flying lessons herself. Jackie suggested that women pilots could help in a war by taking over military flying jobs that didn't involve fighting so male pilots could be released for combat service. Mrs. Roosevelt liked the idea and later wrote in a newspaper article that women pilots were "a weapon waiting to be used." But the Army wasn't interested.

Jackie didn't give up. In March 1941, she met the head of flying for the Army, General Henry "Hap" Arnold. The United States still wasn't in the war but was sending warplanes to Britain for British fliers to use against Hitler. General Arnold asked Jackie to deliver a twin-engine bomber. A woman had never flown a bomber "across the pond" (pilot slang for "across the Atlantic Ocean"). Some men pilots didn't think she could do it, but she did. She wasn't allowed to handle takeoff or landing, but she helped fly that big bomber across the Atlantic from Canada to an air base in Scotland. When she returned home, President and Mrs. Roosevelt invited Jackie to lunch. A few days later, the President arranged for Jackie to find out how many other American women could fly well enough to handle military planes.

JACQUELINE COCHRAN

HALL OF FAMER

CLOSE-UP

Jackie Cochran set more speed, distance, and altitude records than any other pilot of her time, male or female—even more than her friend Amelia Earhart.

Jackie and Amelia met in 1935 when they entered a famous air race—the Bendix Trophy Race—that until two years before had been only for men.

Neither woman won in 1935. But in 1938, Jackie won first prize, beating every man in the race.

That was the first of many victories. As General Hap Arnold noted, she "several times had won air races from men who are now general officers of the Air Forces." She also won an award for being best woman flier of the year 15 times. In 1953, she was the first woman to break the sound barrier, flying faster than the speed of sound. In 1971, nine years before her death, Jackie became one of the first women inducted into the Aviation Hall of Fame.

THUMBS DOWN!

Jackie checked government records and found that almost 3,000 women had pilot's licenses. During the summer of 1941, she wrote up a plan for how they could help the Army. She wanted the most experienced pilots to start flying noncombat missions right away. The less experienced would receive extra training at a school she would set up so they, too, would be ready to fly military planes. General Arnold turned down her plan. He felt he had enough men pilots. But he promised that if he started a women's unit, he would put Jackie in charge.

In the meantime, he suggested she take some American women to England to join the British women's pilot group that was already flying noncombat missions for Britain. So Jackie headed off to Britain with 25 women pilots. If they did a great job, that might persuade the U.S. Army to use women pilots, too.

NANCY LOVE

NANCY'S LETTER

Nancy Love had also been doing research on women pilots. In 1940, when she was in her mid-20s, she wrote to Army officials, suggesting that a small group of about 50 very experienced women pilots could ferry planes for the Army. ("Ferry" means to deliver planes from one place to another.) The Army wasn't interested in her plan, either.

Although not as famous as Jackie, Nancy was an excellent pilot who had been flying since her teens. As a doctor's daughter growing up in Michigan, Nancy went to private schools and had other opportunities Jackie didn't have. At age 16, Nancy learned to fly by taking lessons from a barnstormer. She quit Vassar College after two years and set out to find work as a pilot. She landed several flying jobs, including testing new aircraft equipment. She married a young pilot, Bob Love, and started an aircraft sales company in Boston, while still hoping the Army would change its mind about women pilots.

THUMBS UP!

What changed the Army's mind? Japan's surprise attack on Pearl Harbor on December 7, 1941. This caused the United States to go to war with Japan and its ally Germany. The United States faced battles in Asia, the South Pacific, Europe, and North Africa. The country wasn't ready. It didn't have enough planes. Factories worked night and day to make thousands of new planes, which then had to be delivered to air bases and battle-fronts. The Army didn't have enough men to fly combat missions and also deliver new planes.

The pilot shortage grew so bad that things became confused. The part of the Army that handled delivering planes had a new leader, Colonel William Tunner. He was so new to the job that he hadn't heard of Nancy's plan—or Jackie's, either. He found out about Nancy's flying abilities by chance one day while talking with her husband, who had been called up for military service. Colonel Tunner thought Nancy could help him find pilots to solve his problems. He met with her, and a short time later, in June 1942, she gave him her plan for a women's plane-delivery service. This time, the Army rushed to put Nancy's plan into action. On September 10, 1942, the Army announced the creation of Nancy's unit: the WAFS—Women's Auxiliary Ferrying Squadron.

In all the rush, nobody had told Jackie. She was in England finishing up her job of helping Americans join the British women's pilot group. Jackie returned to the United States on the same day that news of Nancy's squadron hit the newspapers. Imagine Jackie's shock when she read that a women's squadron was starting and she wasn't the head of it!

Jackie met with General Arnold and worked out a compromise. Nancy's squadron would start—and so would Jackie's training program, which at first was called the WFTD—Women's Flying Training Detachment (nicknamed the "Woofteddies"). Her training school would give women pilots the extra skills they needed to fly military planes.

NANCY LOVE

ALWAYS FLYING

CLOSE-UP

After the United States entered the war, Nancy Love and her husband moved to Washington, D.C., where he was working for the Army Air Forces. Nancy found a job in an Army office in Baltimore, Maryland, planning routes male pilots would use in delivering Army planes. Nancy didn't fly on this job, but she flew to it. Instead of driving a car to her Baltimore office, she flew there each day in a plane she owned.

When her WAFS squadron started, and later when she became head of ferry pilots for the WASPs, Nancy kept on flying. "Nancy flew just like we did," explains Barbara Erickson London, one of Nancy's pilots. "Every type of airplane we flew, Nancy flew it first."

Nancy didn't want to run a big air corps, as Jackie Cochran did, and wasn't always happy with Jackie's ideas. "Nancy wasn't one to be bitter," says Florene Miller Watson. "She would not want to do anything to undercut Jackie, or the WASPs. She just went ahead and did what they wanted her to do. She was always a 'lady.' She loved to fly, she really did."

WASPS AT LAST

Both Nancy's and Jackie's programs were up and running by the end of 1942. The next year, in the summer of 1943, these two program were combined into one big group with a snazzier name: WASPs—Women Airforce Service Pilots.

WASPs not only delivered planes but flew many other kinds of noncombat missions. Jackie, now in her mid-30s, was the head of the whole WASP program. Nancy, age 29, was put in charge of all WASPs who would ferry planes.

Jackie and Nancy didn't always agree, but they tried to stay out of each other's way. Their offices were in different cities. "They never saw much of each other," notes Barbara Erickson London. Nancy ran her part of the program—the plane-delivery service—pretty much on her own. She didn't like being in an office and delivered many planes herself.

Jackie, on the other hand, seemed to like the deal-making that goes with running a large organization. "She was forceful and focused and not everybody liked her," observes B.J. Williams "But you can't always win a popularity contest and be effective." If it weren't for Jackie, the WASP program would not have been as big as it was. She welcomed into the WASPs hundreds of women who had flown only a little before the war. She wanted to run a real women's air corps. Jackie, as Dora Dougherty Strother notes, "fought for us . . . for the concept that she believed in, that women could do this. She probably was the only person that could have done it as effectively."

ONE OF NANCY'S WAFS PILOTS (FAR LEFT) AND ONE OF JACKIE'S TRAINEES (NEAR LEFT)—EAGER TO HELP WITH THE WAR

ROUGH SKIES

However, there was a cloud on the horizon, all because one little word—pilot—was left out of a law Congress passed in 1942. This law created a new women's unit for the Army and listed all the jobs women in this unit could do. "Pilot" wasn't on the list. So legally, women pilots could not be part of the Army's new women's group.

Changing the law could take months. Army officials didn't want to wait. Neither did Jackie or Nancy. To get around the law, it was decided that women pilots would work for the Army without officially being in the Army. That meant the women pilots couldn't have military titles or wear Army uniforms. They weren't covered by Army insurance and were paid less than male pilots who did the same kind of flying.

Jackie and Nancy decided to accept this less-than-perfect arrangement. The war was going badly. Jackie and Nancy felt a big responsibility to have women pilots on the job as soon as possible, so they could help with the war—and also prove their worth.

*FLORENE MILLER WATSON
IN HER WAFS JACKET*

4

READY TO SIGN UP

A telegram arrived in September 1942 at the Texas home of Florene Miller Watson. The telegram came from the Army Air Forces. It invited Florene to join Nancy Love's new squadron, which would deliver planes for the Army. Florene had been flying for two years and was teaching young men to be military pilots. She happily gave up that job to fly military planes herself.

NANCY'S EXPERTS

Florene wasn't at home when her telegram arrived. She was on a vacation in Florida and learned of the telegram when she spoke by phone with her mom. To join the squadron, Florene had to travel right away to the squadron's headquarters at an Army air base in Wilmington, Delaware. "I had only my vacation clothes," Florene recalls. "I didn't care. I took a train to Delaware. Women in World War II were gutsy. When an opportunity came, you got out there and did it."

Only about 80 women were invited to join the squadron—just those who had a lot of flying experience. A few others read about the squadron in newspapers and asked to join. Altogether, 28 women made their way to Delaware to become part of this exciting new adventure.

They had to have flown for at least 500 hours—more than twice as much as was needed for men who did the same job: deliver planes. The women also had to be at least 21 years old and high school graduates. Men, however, could be as young as 19 and didn't have to have graduated from high school.

Many of Nancy's pilots had much more than the required 500 hours of flying time. Teresa James, the former barnstormer, was one of the first to sign up. She had flown more than 2,000 hours. The average for the group was about 1,000 hours. That's a lot of flying—almost as much as the 1,500 hours an airline pilot needs today. Nancy wanted only experts.

BETTY GILLIES

FLYING MOM

CLOSE-UP

As a mom with two young kids, Betty Gillies had a lot of responsibilities to juggle. She had been flying since her teens and was one of the best ferry pilots in Nancy's squadron. Betty was stationed at a base in Delaware but often spent several days at a time staying at the aircraft factory in New York where the planes she delivered were made. This factory was near her home. Every few weeks she was able to see her kids and husband, a pilot who was an executive with an aircraft company. A nanny took care of her son, Pete, and her daughter, Pat, while Betty was away.

"I was about 10 when Mom went into the WASPs," remembers Pete, who became a helicopter pilot when he grew up. "I was very proud of Mom and what she was doing. My friends thought I was the luckiest guy in the world to have a Mom and Dad who flew airplanes, and military airplanes at that!"

He remembers a day his mother took him out to the aircraft factory. "She was scheduled to fly a new P-47 fighter from the factory to some place far away, but the four machine guns had to be test-fired before she could start on the flight." Pete got to fire the guns. The crew chief helped Pete into the pilot's seat, keeping the cockpit roof open. "I was barely able to see over the edge of the cockpit," Pete recalls. "The crew chief was standing on the wing, leaning into the cockpit to tell me what to do. When he gave the order to fire, all I had to do was press a particular button. I thought the world had come to an end. The noise was unbelievable! That had to be the biggest thrill in my 10 years of life. What a great day that was!"

After these expert pilots arrived at the base in Delaware, they had to pass the Army's physical exam to be sure they were strong and healthy. They also had to take flying tests to prove they could handle Army planes. Next, they spent a few weeks learning about Army rules and aircraft. Then they got right to work delivering planes.

At first, these women were called WAFS (Women's Auxiliary Ferrying Squadron). A year later, when Nancy's squadron joined with Jackie Cochran's training program, Nancy's pilots became known as WASPs.

Like Florene, most women in Nancy's first squadron had been working as flight instructors. They could have earned more money if they kept on teaching. But the idea of flying powerful Army planes was hard to resist. "I'd have flown those planes for free," explains Barbara Erickson London. At age 22, Barbara was one of Nancy's youngest pilots. The oldest were in their mid-30s. Some were single; others were married, often with husbands in the armed forces. Teresa married just before signing up, but, sadly, her husband died late in the war when his B-17 bomber was shot down over France.

TERESA JAMES, WITH A PARACHUTE STRAPPED ON

JACKIE'S TRAINEES

Soon after telegrams for Nancy's squadron went out, Jackie Cochran sent out her own telegrams. She invited other women pilots to sign up for her new training program. Although these women knew how to fly, Jackie's program would help prepare them to fly military planes.

Some women, like Gene Shaffer Fitzpatrick, didn't receive telegrams but learned of Jackie's program from magazine articles. "I didn't know about it until I saw an article in *Life* magazine. I thought: 'Oh, doggone, this is the way to go!'" Unlike the very experienced pilots in Nancy's squadron, Gene and most of the other women who applied to join Jackie's program hadn't been earning a living from flying. They had been doing other jobs or were college students. However, a few had aviation jobs. Lois Hollingsworth Ziler had graduated from Purdue University with a degree in aeronautical engineering and had a terrific job designing airplane engines. But when she heard about Jackie's program, she gave up that job to sign up with Jackie. Military planes—and Jackie's fame—were hard to resist.

JACKIE'S TRAINING CENTER WAS THE COVER STORY IN THIS ISSUE OF LIFE MAGAZINE.

CLOSE-UP

GENE SHAFFER FITZPATRICK

BANANA RESCUE

When 23-year-old Gene Shaffer Fitzpatrick applied to join the WASPs in 1943, she feared she might not be accepted because she was too skinny. A WASP had to weigh at least 120 pounds. Right before she drove out to an Army base to have her medical exam, Gene and her mom went to a fancy restaurant in San Francisco and had a huge, seven-course lunch. Then, during the drive to the Army base outside of town, Gene slurped down a bottle of milk and munched a bunch of bananas. That afternoon, as she stood on the Army doctor's scale, the marker just barely reached the 120-pound mark.

"You just got in under the wire," said the doctor.

"Oh, I was on a diet," answered Gene.

GETTING IN

More than 25,000 women applied to join Jackie's training program. However, the requirements for being accepted were tough—much harder than for the pilot training programs the Army had for men. Women had to be pilots already to be accepted into Jackie's program, but men who had never flown at all could enter the training programs for male cadets. At first, Jackie's trainees had to have flown at least 200 hours and be 21 years old. During 1943, the Army lightened up on the requirements. By the end of that year, women could sign up who were as young as 18 and who had flown only 35 hours—the number needed for a beginner's license.

Before being accepted, women had to be interviewed by Jackie or one of her assistants. "I guess they wanted to make sure we didn't have two heads or something," explains Gene. "I was nervous at my interview. There were about eight other girls in the room with me." Each had to show her pilot's license and log book to prove she had flown the right number of hours. "The log book was like a diary," explains Nonie Horton Anderson. When a pilot soloed, she wrote the time in her log book, and her instructor signed it; pilots do the same today.

Next came a medical exam at an Army base. The women had to pass the same medical exam given to male recruits. Women had to be at least five feet two inches tall, so their feet could reach a plane's pedals. They also had to be strong, because military planes at the time didn't have the automatic features used today. It took a lot of strength to push the foot pedals and to operate the main hand control, called the stick.

Altogether, 1,830 women passed all these requirements and were accepted into Jackie's training program. More than half of those accepted—1,074—completed the training successfully. Like Nancy's pilots, many of Jackie's trainees had brothers, fathers, or husbands in the armed forces. These women were eager to do their part.

ON THEIR WAY

After being accepted into Jackie's training program, the women had to make their way down to Texas, where the WASP training center was located. A few women drove, but most went by train. "I remember standing up or sitting on my suitcase the whole way. I didn't get a seat," says Maggie Gee, who took a train from her home in northern California. "Trains were hard to get on at the time. There were so many soldiers being moved about on the trains. I had never been that far away from home before. It's not like now, when everyone travels so much. I was nervous. I was excited, too, and wondered what it was going to be like."

MAGGIE GEE, WAITING TO FLY

Left Out

Few minority women served in the WASPs. There were two Asian Americans, including Maggie Gee, and one Native American, but no African Americans. The armed forces were still segregated. African Americans couldn't serve in the same units, sleep in the same barracks, or eat at the same tables with whites. The Army set up a special base in Tuskegee, Alabama, to give pilot training to about 900 African-American men, but not to any African-American women.

Jackie Cochran discouraged African Americans from joining the WASPs. She felt that fighting prejudice against women pilots was hard enough without also battling race discrimination. She feared this extra problem might make the Army end the WASP program. "It's a terrible thing to say, but things were that way then," explains Maggie.

Several black women applied. Some didn't have enough flying experience. Even those who did weren't accepted. "I was

JANET HARMON BRAGG

refused because of the color of my skin," concluded Janet Harmon Bragg in her autobiography, *Soaring Above Setbacks.* "After this rejection I was upset. I knew I could fly. I even had my own plane!" Janet had been flying for several years and had helped start a flying school and an organization for black pilots in Chicago. After her WASP rejection, she focused on her nursing career but was honored in 1982 by the National Air and Space Museum for her earlier contributions to aviation.

"Luckily, it's different now," notes Maggie. After the war, in 1948, President Harry Truman ended segregation in the armed forces. Today, people of any race can serve as equals in all branches of the military.

"I WAS SCARED FROM THE DAY I STARTED IN TRAINING UNTIL I GRADUATED," RECALLS FAITH BUCHNER RICHARDS, SECOND WOMAN FROM THE LEFT IN THIS GROUP OF WASP TRAINEES. "I JUST DIDN'T KNOW WHETHER I WAS GOING TO MAKE IT." BUT SHE DID.

WASH-OUT WORRIES

"You are very badly needed." That's what Jackie Cochran told the first class of 30 women pilots on the day in November 1942 when they began training at the school she had set up in Texas. Then came a no-nonsense warning from the Army officer in charge of the training center, Captain Paul Garrett: "If you think you're hot pilots, I'd advise you to forget it. You are here to learn to fly the way the Army flies."

TOUGH TRAINING

He listed several ways the women could "wash out" (pilot slang for "flunk"). Not only might they have to leave the program if they did poorly in their classwork or failed too many flight tests, they could also wash out if they misbehaved or didn't obey Army rules. "The whole time I was in training I thought I was going to wash out every day," recalls Gene Shaffer Fitzpatrick, who was in one of the later classes.

Every few weeks a new class of women pilots arrived to start this tough training. Many classes had more than one hundred students. Altogether, 18 classes took the training, spending from five to six months learning to "fly the Army way."

Even though training was tough and the women worried about washing out, they loved the challenge. "I'm so happy here," Marjorie Osborne Nicol wrote in a letter home to her mom. "Last night one of the girls and I walked all over the field and every once in a while we'd just stop and pinch each other to make sure we were really here."

THE ARMY WAY

Jackie's trainees received nearly the same kind of military pilot training that male cadets received. The women's course was a little shorter than the men's, partly because women didn't need to learn combat skills, such as how to fire a plane's guns. The women could also skip the beginning flying lessons that men took because WASPs already knew how to fly. Other than that, WASPs covered pretty much the same material as the men and did as well, too. The percentage of students who finished training successfully was the same for women as for men.

"They kept us busy," recalls Gene. Trainees rose at 6:00 a.m., had breakfast, and were ready for action by 7:00 a.m. Half of each day was spent on flying. For the rest of the day, trainees went to "ground school," taking classes in subjects such as physics, weather, maps, and the science of flying. They learned navigation skills so they could find their way through the sky and studied math to do the calculations needed to plan routes. After a 7:00 p.m. dinner, there was homework and studying for tests. Then it was lights out at 10:00 p.m. "It was excellent training," says Gene. "It taught me the fine art of flying."

DURING TRAINING, HALF OF EACH DAY WAS SPENT ON FLYING (ABOVE, LEFT). THIS STUDENT IS PICKING UP A FEW TIPS FROM HER INSTRUCTOR.

THE OTHER HALF OF THE DAY WAS SPENT IN CLASSES LEARNING THE SCIENCE OF FLYING AND EVEN TAKING APART A PLANE'S ENGINE (ABOVE, RIGHT).

FIFI DECORATED THE GATE AT THE ENTRANCE TO THE WASP TRAINING CENTER IN SWEETWATER, TEXAS.

FOG, SAND, AND SNAKES

It's amazing that Jackie's first classes did well, because their first training center was less than wonderful. Jackie had only two months to set up her school. The only place she could find for it was some buildings at Houston's Municipal Airport. However, there were no barracks at the airport where women could live; they had to stay at nearby motels, some of which were run-down. There wasn't a wide variety of planes at the airport for students to use for practicing. Even worse was the thick fog that rolled in from the Gulf of Mexico, often making it impossible to fly.

In April 1943, Jackie persuaded the Army to move the training center to Avenger Field in Sweetwater, Texas. This air base was deep in the heart of west Texas, hundreds of miles from the foggy coast. The base had been used to train male pilots and had classrooms, barracks, and plenty of planes. The last male students soon left, and the women had the base to themselves.

Skies over the new training center at Avenger Field were clear much of the time, and the land was flat, making it a great place to fly. However, there were a few drawbacks. "It was very desolate," recalls Maggie Gee. "Sweetwater today is different. It's quite green. Back then it was a desert." Faith Buchner Richards adds that "the wind blew all the time and you had to learn

how to adjust to that." Marjorie joked in a letter to her mom that "everything looks pretty dusty around here . . . the food is excellent and in between meals we chew dust."

It was very hot in the summer, and cold and snowy in the winter. "There were scorpions," notes Nonie Horton Anderson. "Big ones. When you hit them with a shoe, they made a crack." There were also black widow spiders, tarantulas, and rattlesnakes. Before climbing into a plane, WASPs checked cockpits to be sure a rattler hadn't slithered in for a nap. But those snakes didn't stop some daring WASPs from carrying their beds outside on hot Texas nights to try to cool off, because the barracks had no fans or air conditioners. However, one night, "in the light of the stars, some of them saw a snake slithering over near a group of girls sleeping," according to Marty Wyall, who felt very relieved when the snake was killed.

Fear of those rattlers led the women to choose sturdy shoes for flying—shoes that could be strapped on or tied snugly so they wouldn't fall off if a woman had to parachute out of a plane. "The hot desert was not something you wanted to walk through barefoot," explains Elaine Danforth Harmon, "because of the rattlesnakes and the heat."

31

ZOOT SUITS

Besides snug-fitting shoes, trainees wore huge overalls while flying. The Army provided these overalls, but they came only in men's sizes. Faith notes they were either "big or too big . . . you were swallowed up by them . . . you wound the belt around your waist a couple of times. . . ." WASPs called the overalls zoot suits, after baggy suits popular with some men at the time. The Army also supplied each WASP with a leather jacket.

When not flying, the trainees wore their own clothes. They didn't have Army uniforms because they weren't officially in the Army. For special occasions, the women tried to buy clothes that looked like uniforms. Jackie's trainees bought khaki pants and white shirts for graduations; many wore these outfits after they graduated and were on the job. The pilots in Nancy's plane-delivery units bought gray suits. Finally, in the spring of 1944,

about a year and a half after Jackie's and Nancy's programs started, Jackie persuaded the Army to give all the women pilots their own special uniform, good-looking suits in a dark blue called Santiago blue.

NONIE HORTON ANDERSON (NEAR RIGHT) AND MICKY AXTON, SHOWING OFF THE TRAINEES' HUGE "ZOOT SUITS"

ARMY RULES

Although they couldn't wear Army uniforms, the women had to obey Army rules. They lived in buildings called barracks that were divided into many two-room units. Each room had about six beds. Between the two rooms was a small bathroom that all 12 women in that unit shared. Beds had to be made Army style. Elaine explains, "You had to get the blanket and sheets on the bed so tight a quarter would bounce off it." Lois Hollingsworth Ziler recalls, "I made it and never slept in it again." Instead, she slept on top of the blanket. "I saved a lot of time that way," she adds.

Barracks had to be super clean for Saturday morning inspection, when Army officers wearing white gloves checked to see if the rooms were spotless. "If one gal left an apple in her locker, we all got demerits, not just the one who broke the rule," recalls B.J. Williams. She notes that if a trainee had more than 70 demerits, she had to leave the WASPs.

Like real soldiers, WASPs marched everywhere. One of their marching instructors taught them an old Army saying that helped them survive the toughest days: "If the Army can dish it out, I can take it."

CHALLENGING PLANES

"How wonderful," thought Nancy Johnson when she saw the PT-19, the first plane she would fly in WASP training. "It's so fast and strong and . . . powerful." Before entering the WASPs, most of the trainees had flown only small planes, like Piper Cubs. The PT-19, with its 175-horsepower engine and a top speed of about 130 miles per hour, was more than twice as powerful as a Cub.

The PT-19 was a training plane. That's what the "PT" in its name meant: "primary trainer." Each PT-19 had two cockpits. A student sat in the front cockpit, and an instructor sat in the back cockpit, helping with the controls and giving advice through a tube connected to a student's helmet or earphones. After several sessions, a student had to fly the plane on her own, while the teacher sat in the back watching. If the student did well, she could then take up the plane all by herself.

Cockpits on the PT-19 had no roof. They were totally open to the air. If the plane turned over and the pilot's seat belt wasn't fastened, she could fall out. A few did,

but they landed safely, thanks to their parachutes. That made them eligible for the "Caterpillar Club," named for the tiny creature that made the silk used in their parachutes. This club, which started in the 1920s, is for pilots who make emergency parachute jumps from their planes.

TO KEEP MAPS FROM BLOWING OUT OF AN OPEN-COCKPIT PT-19, WASPS STRAPPED THEM TO THEIR LEGS. THEY ALSO STUCK TAPE ON THE LEGS OF THEIR "ZOOT SUITS" TO HAVE SOMETHING TO WRITE ON WHILE FLYING (SEE PHOTOS PAGES 21, 34–35, AND 42).

TRAINEES MARCHING TO CLASS AROUND THE WISHING WELL AT AVENGER FIELD

A BT-13 TRAINER, UNLIKE A PT-19, HAD A COCKPIT ROOF THAT COULD SLIDE SHUT.

After a WASP conquered open-air trainers like the PT-19 and PT-17, she moved on to more powerful planes: the 450-horsepower BT-13 Valiant and the 600-horsepower AT-6 Texan. These offered a less breezy ride because they had a roof that could slide over the cockpit.

Marjorie noted in a letter after her first ride in an AT-6, "As I climbed into the cockpit my heart sank. I don't see how I can possibly learn all of those 'things' on the instrument board. . . . The actual flying will be simple; it's the cockpit procedure, the take-off procedure, and all the rest of the procedures that knock you over."

After learning how to operate these single-engine planes, WASPs tackled a plane with two engines, the AT-17 Cessna Bobcat. It was nicknamed the "Bamboo Bomber" because it was made largely of plywood and canvas.

WASPs learned how to handle each plane in all kinds of situations. They practiced making emergency landings and doing lazy-eights, loops, and slow rolls. They also learned how to make a plane fly again if it stalled in midair or went into a spin, which would send it spiraling down toward the ground. To master this skill, they first made a plane go into a spin, and then worked the plane's controls quickly to get out of the spin before the plane could crash. According to Marty, "At first it scared me silly to do a spin, but after doing some every day for a couple of weeks I've lost my tenseness."

NO PEEKING

WASPs also trained on something that looked like a toy airplane, the Link Trainer. It never left the ground. Instead, it sat inside a classroom. Pilots trained on the Link to learn to fly using only a plane's instruments. It was important to know how to fly without having to look out a cockpit window. That's a skill pilots need for those times when it's so cloudy or dark that looking out the window won't help. Inside the Link was a regular cockpit, and a student used its instruments and controls to "fly." A teacher sitting nearby gave commands, which the student heard through earphones. A special recording pen hooked up to the Link kept track of the student's "flight" on a chart.

After practicing with the Link, WASPs flew a real plane the same way—using only its instruments. The cockpit window where the student sat was blocked with a "hood," a black piece of canvas. She couldn't see out the window, but she still could see the instrument panel. Sara Chapin Winston explained in a letter to her mom: "I sit in the rear, pull up a black cloth hood and fly the darn thing on instruments alone while he [the instructor] sits up front and watches for other planes, tells me where to go and tries to keep me from killing us both." Flying without being able to see the ground confuses your body; you feel as if you're going one way when you're really going the other. According to Marjorie, "It's an odd sensation—you can't trust your sensations at all—only those instruments in front of you." After mastering "under the hood" flying, WASPs flew at night, when it's really hard to tell where the sky ends and the ground begins.

A WASP SITTING ON A LINK TRAINER

Flight Note	
ALPHABET SOUP: Here's what the initials in the planes' names meant:	
PT	Primary Trainer
BT	Basic Trainer
AT	Advanced Trainer
P	Pursuit (fighter)
B	Bomber
A	Assault
C	Cargo

HEADING OUT IN AN AT-6

*PLOTTING THE ROUTE
BEFORE A TRIP*

TAKING A TRIP

Toward the end of training, WASPs practiced flying cross-country, first with an instructor and later going solo. They didn't fly all the way across the United States—just an hour or two away from Sweetwater. They had to find their way to an unfamiliar airfield, land there, and then fly home.

Today, pilots on big planes find their way by using computers and other equipment, including receivers that bounce information off satellites. World War II pilots didn't have such fancy gear. Many planes didn't even have radios. Pilots often had only a map, a compass, and a watch.

Before a cross-country trip, WASPs used a flight map to plan their route. They drew straight lines on the map from their starting point to where they were going. They calculated what speed and altitude to use, taking into account air currents and wind speed. They checked weather reports to know what conditions they might meet along the way.

The maps noted big objects on the ground that a pilot could see from the air, such as water towers, railroad tracks, or ponds. A pilot picked several objects along her route as checkpoints. She calculated how long it would take to fly from one to the next. Once in the air, she used her compass to be sure she flew in the right direction. She checked her watch to see if she passed each checkpoint on time.

"If you do not find the checkpoint on the ground that matches your map after you've flown the right number of minutes, you know you're off course," explains Florene Miller Watson, one of Nancy Love's pilots. To get back on course, a pilot searched the map for landmarks she could see on the ground. Then she figured out how long it would take to go from where she was to her next checkpoint. "Sometimes maps did not match what you saw on the ground because things on the ground may have changed," adds Florene. So she paid close attention to something that usually didn't change—the squiggly contour lines on a map that show how hilly the ground is.

Flying this way is called using VFR (Visual Flight Rules), something beginning pilots today also learn. WASPs joked that if they became really lost, they could use IFR ("I follow the railroad"). If they saw railroad tracks down below, they flew along them to the next town, and then looked for landmarks to identify what town it was.

In planes that had a radio, pilots could "fly the beam," using signals that radio towers beamed out and that a pilot could hear over her radio. These signals helped her know where she was.

Some WASPs got a little lost on their first cross-country trips, as happened to most pilots until they got the hang of navigating. Soon the women learned to find their way.

CHECK OUT OR WASH OUT

All through training, students were constantly tested, not only in the classroom but also in the air. They had to take flight tests, called "check rides," for each kind of plane they learned to fly. They had to "check out," or pass, check rides on one type of plane before moving on to the next plane in the training series. They also had to pass check rides for special skills, such as night flying or flying using instruments only.

On check rides, the student flew the plane while an examiner in the plane called out things for the student to do. First, she had to pass a check ride with a civilian instructor as the examiner. Then came a check ride with an Army officer as the tester. If a student flunked a check ride, she could try again later. But if she failed twice with an Army officer, she "washed out" and had to leave the WASPs.

Most students passed their Army check rides. For those who washed out, part of the problem may have been the program's fast pace. "I think it wasn't whether you were smart enough or capable enough. It was that you had to be able to learn fast," explains Bernice Falk Haydu. Teacher troubles may have caused a few washouts. "We were told at the very beginning it will not be held against you if you say that you would like another instructor," notes Bernice.

The instructors were civilians. Some instructors were women, but most were men. A few of them didn't like teaching women and could be mean. Luckily, most teachers were helpful, such as Kenneth Eckley, who reported, "I was probably like all the rest of the men pilots, wasn't sure they [WASPs] could fly . . . but still it turned out very well. I've had women pilots that were . . . better . . . than any man pilot that I flew with."

CLOSE-UP

MARJORIE OSBORNE NICOL

"I'M NOT QUITTING"

"Sometimes I'm very discouraged about my flying, but everyone else is, too. We all seem to be of the opinion that we'll wash before we even solo," Marjorie Osborne Nicol wrote her mom after the first weeks of training. A week later she added, "It's all given to us so darned fast. I lie awake nights going over the procedure for every maneuver. . . . Two kids quit today because they're so discouraged. . . . I'm not quitting; I'll give it everything I've got."

Several weeks later she wrote, "I had my Army check and flunked it. . . . I'm to be given a new instructor . . . and another Army check with a different man." Two days later, she took the test again and wrote her mom, " . . . as I climbed into the plane this afternoon with tears practically rolling down my cheeks, they all had their fingers crossed for me." This time Marjorie passed! "I knew I had to do it."

Meeting each new challenge gave Marjorie and the other women a great sense of accomplishment. As Marjorie wrote her mom a few weeks before graduation: "Remember that morning that I left for the WASPs? . . . As we stood in the living room alone saying goodbye to each other, I felt like such a little girl, saying goodbye to home and to family. Today I don't know if I feel grown-up or not—I think that the day I get my wings will do that—but I feel as though I've come along some of the way to growing up, since that morning when I cried in your arms."

WASP TRAINEES FOOLING AROUND

GOOD TIMES, FUN STUFF

6

Training wasn't all hard work, as Marjorie Osborne Nicol discovered. "I've never laughed so much in all my life—these kids are a scream. I love 'em, every one of 'em. . . . we're like sisters to each other." That's how she described her WASP roommates in a letter to her mom. WASP trainees studied hard but also found time to make friends and have fun.

SOARING SONGS

"We all wrote songs," recalls B.J. Williams. "We'd sit with our backs against the hangar, waiting to go flying, and make up a new song." They wrote new words for tunes such as "Deep in the Heart of Texas." In some songs they joked about things like their zoot suits or did a little bragging, as in a song that started: "I'm a flying wreck a riskin' my neck and a helluva pilot too!"

They had time to sing out on the "flight line" (near the runway where planes are parked) because there was only one flight instructor for every four trainees. One at a time, each WASP went up with the instructor for an hour of flying, fitting in about two such flying sessions a day. While waiting for their turn to fly, trainees sat outside near the hangar or in the hangar's "ready room," where they would study, "hangar-fly" (talk about flying), or sing. They also sang as they relaxed in their barracks or as they marched to class or to the mess hall for meals.

WASPS HANG OUT IN A READY ROOM AT AVENGER FIELD. AN INSTRUCTOR USES A MODEL PLANE TO SHOW HOW TO DO A "SLOW ROLL."

41

SUNBATHING BETWEEN THE BARRACKS AT AVENGER FIELD IN
SWEETWATER, TEXAS. (NOTICE WHAT THEY USED FOR BEACH CHAIRS.)

"WHENEVER A TRAINEE SOLOED IN A PLANE FOR THE FIRST TIME, SHE GOT THROWN INTO
THE WISHING WELL," B.J. WILLIAMS REPORTS. IT WAS A WAY TO COOL OFF A "HOT" PILOT.

PRANKS, PLAYS, AND PAPERS

"Some gals pulled gags, like in summer camp. Playful stuff," recalls B.J. "They'd short-sheet your bed. One time they put toothpaste all over my pillow." One hot July night, Caro Bayley Bosca and a roommate "had an ice water fight, getting ourselves, all the beds and occupants practically drenched" and then had to "sleep in drenched sheets."

Some stunts were risky, such as sunbathing while flying in an open-cockpit PT-19. One daredevil even took off her shirt. Male pilots flying nearby saw her and waved. She became so flustered that her shirt flew out of the cockpit. When she landed, she asked some of the other WASPs to bring her a blanket.

One class put on a play, "The Eager Beaver Show," with funny skits about being a WASP trainee. Some women wrote a newspaper. At first it was called *The Fifinella Gazette*, but after the training center moved to Avenger Field, the paper was called *The Avenger*. It had movie reviews, flying tips, and news about the war. Early issues included tall tales about Fifi. Even Jackie Cochran made up a story for the paper about a sprite that supposedly pulled pranks on her.

TIME OFF

"We would have Sundays off, maybe Saturdays, too. We would usually go into Sweetwater and go to the movies or walk around town or go shopping, have a soda," recalls Bernice Falk Haydu. They could picnic at a nearby lake or swim in the town pool. Townspeople sometimes invited WASPs for Sunday supper. The town gave them a room over a store for the Avengerette Club, where WASPs could play records and dance. A few WASPs had cars to use for day trips, and some took bus trips to a local rodeo. "There wasn't much to do," Bernice adds. Maggie Gee points out, "We didn't have time for many extracurricular activities anyway."

They also didn't have much time for dating. At Avenger Field, the only men were instructors, and they were strictly off-limits. "We couldn't date our instructors. If you did, you'd get dismissed instantly," notes B.J.

But Elaine Danforth Harmon adds, "Of course, secretly some of the women did date the instructors, but that was really a no-no."

At first, male pilots from nearby bases pretended to have engine trouble while flying over Avenger Field and made "emergency landings" so they could meet the women. One day, nearly 40 pilots did that. So Jackie had the Army forbid planes from other bases from landing at Avenger Field. This earned the field the nickname "Cochran's Convent." Sometimes the Army brought over male cadets for a Saturday night dance. But as Marjorie wrote in a letter home, "I'm so busy during the week I never think about men—Saturday nights I'd like dates but I really don't care one way or the other. . . . The only thing I want is my silver wings."

JACKIE COCHRAN (CENTER) SHARING FLYING TIPS WITH HER TRAINEES

WASP Songs

Tune: "Home on the Range"

Oh, I'm far from home
Where the wild Texans roam,
Where the snakes and tarantulas play,
Where seldom is heard
An encouraging word
And we never have time to make hay.

A WASP trainee am I—
All sunburned and dusty and dry.
There's no time to play,
They work us all day,
Volunteers, but we'll never know why!

If I graduate
I'll get out of this state
And never see Texas no more—
We'll ferry their planes
Through the wind and the rains
And help all our boys win the war.

Tune: "Deep in the Heart of Texas"

We damn near freeze
In these open PTs
Deep in the heart of Texas.

We're never at our ease
In these big BTs
Deep in the heart of Texas.

If you don't lock the latch,
You'll fall out of the hatch
Deep in the heart of Texas.

If you don't relax
You'll be in *Air Facts**
Deep in the heart of Texas.

*Air Facts was an aviation magazine.

A TRAINEE CHECKS THE SCHEDULE BOARD TO SEE HOW LONG SHE'LL HAVE TO WAIT "JUST FOR A CHANCE TO FLY."

Tune: "I've Been Working on the Railroad"

I've been waiting on the flight line, just for a chance to fly,
I've been waiting on the flight line, for an hour in the sky,
Can't you hear the props a-roaring, warming up on the line
Can't you hear the ships a-calling, come Fifinella, fly.

Tune: "Yankee Doodle"

We are Yankee Doodle Pilots,
Yankee Doodle, do or die!

Real, live nieces of our Uncle Sam,
Born with a yearning to fly.

Keep in step to all our classes
March to flight line with our pals.

Yankee Doodle came to Texas
Just to fly the PTs!

We are those Yankee Doodle Gals.

A PROUD JACKIE (WEARING FLOWERS) LOOKS ON AS A NEW WASP RECEIVES HER WINGS ON GRADUATION DAY.

THE BEST DAY OF ALL: GRADUATION

Of course, the most fun day of all for Jackie's trainees was graduation day. Finally they could stop worrying about washing out. Graduation ceremonies were big events. An Army officer gave a speech, and Jackie was usually there. Sometimes even General Hap Arnold came. A few proud parents sat in the audience, watching their daughters receive their silver wing pins.

The WASPs' wing pins weren't the same ones that male Army pilots received, because WASPs weren't officially in the Army. Jackie used her own money to buy silver wing pins for the first few classes and had a jeweler engrave each class's number in the center of the pin. Eventually she persuaded the Army to provide wings made especially for WASPs.

After graduation, these silver-winged WASPs set out for Army air bases around the country. Graduates from the first few classes joined the pilots in Nancy Love's plane-delivery squadron. Later classes took on other kinds of noncombat flying missions. They all were eager to prove that no matter what kind of mission the Army dished out, they could take it.

SILVER WASP WINGS

GRADUATES OF ONE OF THE LATER WASP CLASSES IN THEIR SANTIAGO BLUE UNIFORMS

47

PILOTS PREPARING TO DELIVER OPEN-COCKPIT PT-19 PLANES

7

SKY-HIGH DELIVERY SERVICE

Months before Jackie Cochran's first class graduated, pilots in Nancy Love's squadron were hard at work delivering planes. "We had to deliver the goods or else. Or else there wouldn't ever be another chance for women pilots in any part of the service." That's how Cornelia Fort, one of Nancy's pilots, sized up the situation.

Because the Army didn't have enough planes when it entered the war, factories were making thousands of new planes each month. "All those new planes had to be moved someplace," explains Barbara Erickson London. Ferry pilots did the moving, taking new planes from the factories where they were made and flying them to air bases or ports around the country. Many planes then went directly to battle zones in Europe or Asia, to be used by U.S. troops.

ON-TIME DELIVERY

At first, the Army wasn't sure women could fly its planes. It gave Cornelia, Barbara, and the others in Nancy's first WAFS squadron three months to prove themselves. If they could deliver planes safely and on time, they could stay on as part of the Army's delivery team. If they messed up, that would be the end of their squadron and maybe also of Jackie's program.

For the squadron's first mission in late October 1942, six of the women delivered some of the Army's smallest planes—Piper Cubs. That's the only kind of plane Army officials let the women ferry pilots fly at first. An Army plane took Cornelia, Betty Gillies, Teresa James, and three others from their home base in Delaware to

an aircraft factory in Pennsylvania. Each woman climbed into a brand-new Cub and flew it to an air base in New York—arriving safely and on time.

Soon Nancy's other pilots flew to bases all over the country, delivering Cubs. These planes were nicknamed "Grasshoppers." The Army used Cubs to train pilots and fly people from place to place. After a delivery, the women hurried back to Delaware by train or bus or by taking an airline flight. They flew so well that the Army let them ferry bigger planes: open-cockpit PT-19 and PT-17 trainers.

The women delivered these larger planes as well as men ferry pilots did—sometimes even better. On one mission, the women came out way on top, as six of them joined 17 male pilots in delivering a group of PT-17s. The mission began with the women and men taking a two-day train ride from Delaware to Montana. There they each took an open-cockpit PT-17 and set out to fly the planes to an air base in Tennessee. By the second day, all six women began landing at the Tennessee base, but most of the men hadn't arrived. After another two days, 11 men still hadn't made it. They either got lost or had trouble with their planes. Some may have stopped for a visit along the way.

The women's outstanding performance convinced the Army not only that the women should keep flying but also that they should be allowed to fly bigger planes. Officials soon spread the women out to other bases.

Betty and Teresa were among those who stayed at New Castle Army Air Base in Wilmington, Delaware. The rest set up new women's ferrying units at bases located near aircraft factories. Cornelia, Barbara, and several others moved to an Army air base in Long Beach, California; Florene Miller Watson was among those who went to a base at Love Field in Dallas, Texas; another group set up a unit in Romulus, Michigan.

By the spring of 1943, the first graduates from Jackie's training program started joining the women's ferrying units. For a while all these plane-delivering women were called WAFS. Later that summer, Jackie's and Nancy's programs joined to form the WASPs. After that, all the women pilots became known as WASPs. However, Cornelia, Betty, Teresa, Barbara, Florene, and the others from Nancy's first squadron called themselves the "Originals." They were the experts who led the way.

CLIMBING INTO A FIGHTER PLANE WASN'T EASY.

FOUR FERRY PILOTS
WITH A P-47 THUNDERBOLT
FIGHTER PLANE

WHAT THEY DELIVERED

Nancy wanted women ferry pilots to be able to deliver all kinds of planes. So she set out to fly some of the Army's most powerful planes, to prove they weren't too difficult for a woman. In early 1943, Nancy learned to fly the Army's new fighter plane, the P-51 Mustang. The "P" in its name meant it was one of the Army's pursuit fighters—one-pilot planes built for scrappy air battles. These single-engine fighters acted as protectors for big bombers, flying alongside to fight off enemy planes. The P-51 was so new that most fighter pilots hadn't flown it yet. Nancy handled it beautifully. Then she checked out in other challenging Army planes.

Betty followed Nancy's lead and learned to fly another fighter—the P-47 Thunderbolt. However, Betty was one of the shortest ferry pilots, and it was hard for her feet to reach the P-47's foot pedals. She put booster blocks on the pedals so her feet could reach—a trick she learned from a short male pilot.

Soon other "Originals" checked out in fighter planes. They had to carry a gun when delivering some fighters that had secret equipment on board that the Army didn't want to fall into enemy hands. If anyone tried to steal the plane, the women were to shoot the fuel tank to blow up the plane. Luckily, they never had to do that.

The women flew so well that by the spring of 1943 the Army announced that all ferry pilots, male or female, could fly any Army plane "to the extent of their ability."

By late 1943, the Army started sending WASPs to special training centers to learn to fly fighters and bombers. Officials realized that WASPs needed to be able to deliver as many kinds of planes as possible because of the invasion of Nazi-controlled Europe that was planned for the next summer. Hundreds of new planes would be needed for that invasion, which would become known as D day.

WASPs didn't deliver planes directly to battle zones. Officials didn't want any women shot down. Instead, WASPs delivered planes to ports and bases in the United States (see map page 59). From there, male pilots flew the bigger planes to the battle zones. Many planes, such as the P-47 and P-51 fighters, couldn't carry enough fuel to make it across the ocean; they went overseas on ships. Sometimes WASPs left notes in the cockpits to wish good luck to the pilots who would fly the planes into battle.

BRRR, IT'S COLD UP THERE

Women also delivered hundreds of PT-19s and other training planes to bases that were preparing young male pilots for battle. According to Cornelia, "Delivering a trainer to Texas may be as important as delivering a bomber to Africa if you take the long view." PT-19s had no radios to help in navigation, though, and their open cockpits made for a very chilly ride. The planes were made in factories up north. Flying through wintry skies in a cockpit open to the wind could make the temperature in the cockpit drop to a frosty 10° F (-12° C). Pilots dressed warmly, wearing woolen underwear under their slacks and shirts. Then came a fur-lined leather flight suit, leather helmet, leather face mask, goggles, and gloves. "The leather suit got so stiff from the cold that when you went to stand up to get out of the plane, you couldn't move very well," recalls Margaret Ray Ringenberg. Sometimes she'd ask the ground crew to "pull me out of here." If a flight headed to a warmer climate, "you could shed one layer," notes Nancy Johnson. "And by the time you got to Florida you were down to just your slacks."

TO KEEP WARM, THE WOMEN WORE BULKY LEATHER FLIGHT SUITS AND BIG BOOTS.

Flight Note

HOLD IT: WASPs didn't have a "relief tube" to use if they had to go to the bathroom while flying. The ones for men didn't work for women. "You just had to control your bladder," says B.J. Williams, by not drinking too many liquids before a flight. "You hoped you could land and get to a ladies' room fast enough." (Today, women pilots use devices designed especially for women.)

BUSY, BUSY, BUSY

"We flew almost every day. Weekends were just like any other day," Barbara explains. "It was first in, first out." If a pilot returned to her home base before midnight, her name was on the list to go out again the next morning. "You went home, took a shower, packed your bag, and were ready to go the following morning." Sometimes the planes they had to deliver were at the base; other times, the women went to a nearby factory to pick up the plane.

With small planes that couldn't fly fast, such as Cubs, it could take several days to deliver them from their Pennsylvania factory to a training base down in Texas. The women usually flew alone in the planes and only during the day, because many planes didn't have the instruments needed for night flying. On bigger planes, like a B-17, they could fly by instruments at night. "But there was no instrument flying with a fighter or anything single-engine, and that's mainly what we were ferrying," notes Barbara.

They had to land before dark, usually at an Army base but sometimes at regular airports. "At a military base,

they nearly always had nurses, and we could bunk in with them. If not, we would go to a hotel," Barbara explains. The Army gave WASPs money for a hotel room—$6 a night, which was what many hotel rooms cost back then.

After a delivery, they returned to their home base as soon as possible. If they were near a city, they took an airline flight. Even if a flight was full, ferry pilots could get a seat. Their work was so important that they could take away a seat from any other passenger, except the President. If WASPs weren't near a city, "we had to take a train or bus to a city to catch an airline flight," recalls Margaret. Trains were crowded. "We had our big B-4 gear bag and our parachute bag, and we'd put our bags down on the floor of the train and curl up on them."

At first the women weren't allowed to fly in military planes with men. But after a while, officials eased up and let women pilots catch a ride in a military plane headed their way. WASPs jokingly called these flights SNAFU Airlines, after a popular Army saying: Situation Normal, All Fouled Up.

TRAVELING LIGHT

Ferry pilots might be away from their home base for days, or even weeks. Barbara remembers one trip that started at her home base in California. First she delivered a plane to New Jersey. "Then they sent me up to Buffalo. I picked up an airplane there and delivered it to Montana. They sent me from there to Kansas City, where I picked up another plane and took it to Alabama, which put me back on the East Coast, and so they sent me up to Long Island for another plane that I took back to California. I was gone a month—with one change of clothes!" This was just one of many long trips Barbara made.

She and the other women carried only one small bag for clothes. "We usually took an extra shirt and a change of underclothes, but not much else because you don't have any place to put it in a fighter plane," Barbara explains. Cockpits were tiny. The women became creative packers. "We rolled up our skirt with the maps and put a shirt in with our paperwork," Barbara says. The pilots needed a skirt because at that time many restaurants wouldn't serve women wearing slacks. They found secret spots to stash stuff. On fighter planes they put high-heeled shoes in empty slots on the wings where bullets would be stored later.

"You learned to wash your shirt every night and iron it over the radiator," Barbara adds. "If the radiator is on and you take a towel and rub it slowly over the top of the shirt over the radiator, you can at least get the collar ironed so it's fairly decent. Of course, the rest of the shirt looked like heck." To "iron" slacks, some WASPs put them under a mattress and slept on them.

Being away from their home base so often made it hard to have much of a social life. "We were just so busy we didn't really think about dating very much," Barbara recalls. WASPs could date only officers because WASPs had to follow the same rules as Army pilots, who were all officers. Army officers can't date anyone in the Army who is not an officer. Barbara dated a young officer, a ferry pilot, whom she met at her base. Because of their busy flying schedules, they often weren't at the base at the same time. There wasn't a lot to do at the base anyway, besides go bowling or see a movie. A few WASPs married during the war, but not Barbara. "I wasn't about to give up my airplanes for marriage," she explains. She and her officer friend did eventually marry—after the war.

MARGARET RAY RINGENBERG

54

SURPRISE LANDINGS

"I landed several places where they couldn't really believe it was a girl flying the airplane until you got on the ground," Barbara recalls. She remembers being in an A-26 over Florida and calling in over the radio to tell the airport tower operators she was ready to land. "They said, 'We don't have you in sight, but we have an A-26 on final approach. Follow that plane.'" Barbara kept calling in, but they didn't realize that she was the one in that A-26 until she landed. She remembers their surprise when they exclaimed, "Oh, look, it's a girl!"

One woman had to make an emergency fueling stop at a base and radioed the tower several times but got no answer. Finally, the tower told her, "Will the lady who is trying to get in and keeps calling, please stay off the air. We're trying to bring in a P-51." She called back, "Tower, the lady on the air is in the P-51."

"A friend of mine flew into a base and they were going to put her in the brig [military jail] for stealing an aircraft. Her commanding officer had to call and say it was okay for her to have that aircraft," recalls Faith Buchner Richards. Even after WASPs had their new Santiago blue uniforms, people still didn't know they were pilots. People thought WASPs might be Red Cross workers, nurses, stewardesses, or even members of the Mexican Army.

However, men pilots who flew with the WASPs knew who they were and respected their flying ability. "Anybody that flew with us was always very good to us," notes Faith. There might be a little jealousy if a woman was flying a bigger plane than a less experienced male pilot. "When they gave us a hard time, I found it better to say nothing and ignore it," notes Margaret. "I'd just leave. That bothered them more than if we would fight back."

"I flew just about every kind of airplane they had," says Florene. "I don't feel I was given anything because I was a girl. Nor do I feel that I was denied anything." Even so, WASPs were under constant pressure to prove what women could do. Florene felt the way to handle that was to "polish your skills, and be ready to take opportunities when they come."

CLOSE-UP

BARBARA ERICKSON LONDON

AIR MEDAL

"I had a fast airplane, the weather was good, and I was able to go straight through on one day, stay overnight, turn around, and come back the other way in one day." That's how Barbara Erickson London describes another of her amazing trips—an 8,000-mile adventure that earned her one of the highest honors given to military pilots: the Air Medal.

Late in the summer of 1943, Barbara made four 2,000-mile trips in just five days of flying, spread over a little more than a week. First, she took a big, new DC-3 from a factory near her home base in California and flew it to a base in Indiana. That base had a new P-47 Thunderbolt that needed to go out to California. So Barbara flew it to California, where she picked up a new P-51 Mustang and flew it back to Indiana. There, she hopped into yet another P-47 and whizzed it back out to California. Whew! "It was a typical example of what a woman ferry pilot did. I never took that medal as a personal honor. It represented what we all did," says Barbara.

FERRY PILOTS CHECKING THEIR MAPS

FLORENE MILLER WATSON

FOLLOW ME

"I got a reputation for being a good navigator, and everybody wanted to follow me," Florene Miller Watson recalls. Often several planes would be delivered on the same day to the same place. Not just WASPs followed Florene. "Guys would want to follow me, too. I'd say, 'I don't care who follows me, but pay attention and don't you all be dumb and sit on your map and not know where you are.' It was kind of a scary business, tooting around up there. We often didn't have anything but a compass, a map, and a watch to figure out how in the heck to get where we were going up there in the big sky. Guys who knew me would say, 'When she gets her lipstick and comb out, you know we're getting close.' Guys kidded me a lot about that. I'd be bouncing all over the sky trying to get my hair done and my lipstick on and get myself organized for landing."

DANGER IN THE SKY

On a sunny day in March 1943, just over a year after Cornelia had watched in horror from the sky as enemy planes bombed Pearl Harbor, she took off from her home base in California. She had to deliver a BT-13 Valiant to Dallas. So did six male pilots, who made the trip with Cornelia. As they flew over west Texas, two of the BT-13s—Cornelia's and one of the men's planes—came too close together. His plane damaged Cornelia's. He was OK and continued on his flight, but Cornelia's plane was so badly damaged that it spun out of control. She died as her plane crashed into the ground. Cornelia became the first woman pilot to die while on active duty, flying a mission for the U.S. armed forces.

Some people wondered if perhaps the male pilot had been fooling around, as hotshot young pilots sometimes did. An Army investigation found it was an accident and nobody was to blame.

Altogether, 38 of the women pilots died, some while on active duty, others while still in training. Equipment problems caused many tragedies. One trainee and her instructor died when their plane crashed because of mechanical problems. Ferry pilots often flew new planes that had never been flown before, and some of the planes developed engine trouble on their first flights. WASPs who flew other missions often used planes that were in such bad shape the engines quit in midair. Poor weather caused some crashes; others happened because of mistakes made by the ground crew, other pilots, or by WASPs themselves. However, the women didn't have more accidents than men doing the same kinds of flying. The WASP safety record was actually a little better than that of the men.

Unfortunately, because these women weren't officially in the military, the Army didn't provide much to the families of women pilots who died. There was no flag for the coffin, no insurance money, no gold star for parents to hang in the window to show that their child had died in the war—all things provided for people who were officially part of the military. The Army didn't pay for anyone to bring home to their families the coffins of Cornelia and other women pilots who died; the women pilots often collected money among themselves for that.

The death of fellow WASPs was upsetting, "but we dared not let our emotions run away with us," explains Dora Dougherty Strother. "After all, men were dying every day in battles in the war. People we had gone to high school with, relatives, and husbands of some of the gals were in the war and were dying." More than 50,000 men in the Army Air Forces died during the war. Dora and the other women understood that flying could be dangerous. But they also knew they were doing important work that would help end the war. They wouldn't let fear stop them.

Cornelia realized flying was risky, too. In a letter to her mom, Cornelia explained how she wanted to be remembered in case she should die in an accident:

"I was happiest in the sky—at dawn when the quietness of the air was like a caress, when the noon sun beat down, and at dusk when the sky was drenched with the fading light. Think of me there and remember me, I hope, as I shall you."

WELL DONE

About 300 women served as ferry pilots, many fewer than the more than 8,000 male ferry pilots. But the women did their share of the work, flying 77 different kinds of planes and making more than 12,000 deliveries. Altogether, men and women made a total of about 312,000 deliveries. By the end of 1944, WASPs were delivering nearly all the Army's fighter planes. Ferry pilots usually flew alone in the cockpit, and to make a delivery on time, they often flew in bad weather. It was hard work, but also exciting. "I had a good time," reports Barbara. "Here I was a girl of 22 given a million-dollar airplane and told, 'Go fly!'"

CORNELIA FORT HANDING OVER PAPERS FOR A PLANE SHE HAD JUST DELIVERED

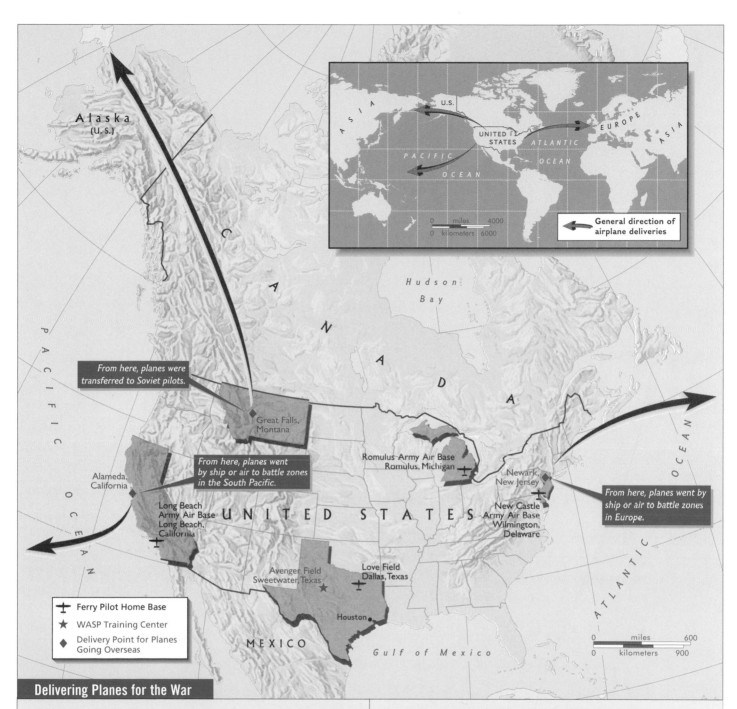

From here, planes were
transferred to Soviet pilots.

From here, planes went
by ship or air to battle zones
in the South Pacific.

From here, planes went by
ship or air to battle zones
in Europe.

Alaska
(U.S.)

C A N A D A

Hudson
Bay

PACIFIC OCEAN

Great Falls,
Montana

Romulus Army Air Base
Romulus, Michigan

Newark,
New Jersey

New Castle
Army Air Base
Wilmington,
Delaware

Alameda,
California

Long Beach
Army Air Base
Long Beach,
California

U N I T E D   S T A T E S

Avenger Field
Sweetwater, Texas

Love Field
Dallas, Texas

Houston

M E X I C O

Gulf of Mexico

ATLANTIC OCEAN

General direction of
airplane deliveries

ASIA   U.S.   EUROPE

UNITED
STATES   ATLANTIC OCEAN

PACIFIC OCEAN   ASIA

0   miles   4000
0   kilometers   6000

✝ Ferry Pilot Home Base

★ WASP Training Center

◆ Delivery Point for Planes
   Going Overseas

0   miles   600
0   kilometers   900

Delivering Planes for the War

This map shows some of the places where women ferry pilots delivered planes and the battle zones the planes went on to. The map also shows the four main home bases for women ferry pilots, and the WASP training center.

Not shown are the hundreds of training bases where women delivered planes that were used to train male pilots. Also not shown are the approximately 120 home bases for WASPs who didn't deliver planes but flew other kinds of missions.

The Army wouldn't let women ferry pilots fly planes out of the United States directly to battle zones. After a woman delivered a plane to Newark, New Jersey, or to Alameda, California, it was transported overseas to a battle zone by ship or was flown there by a male pilot. Planes delivered to Great Falls, Montana, were transferred to Soviet pilots, some of whom were women.

A WASP FLYING AN A-25 HELLDIVER, ONE OF THE
PLANES USED FOR PULLING SKY-HIGH TARGETS

THE HUGE GUN THAT TROOPS ON
THE GROUND AIMED AT CLOTH TARGETS
PULLED BY THE WASPS' PLANES

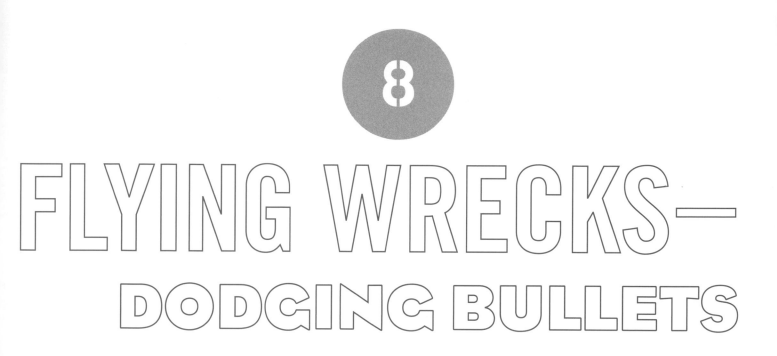

8

FLYING WRECKS—
DODGING BULLETS

"We work with the anti-aircraft ground troops—they practice combat conditions every day in [the] desert and we do whatever they want us to do to make combat conditions," wrote Caro Bayley Bosca in a letter from the Texas air base where she worked as a WASP. She was one of the WASPs who came about as close to being in combat as a woman pilot could. They played the part of enemy pilots in pretend battles to prepare soldiers for what they would face in real fighting.

RISKY BUSINESS

It was risky work. So was the test-flying of repaired airplanes that kept other WASPs busy. "There was a scarcity of planes. The Army needed every plane it could get," explains B.J. Williams. "When a plane was damaged in flight and then repaired, it had to be test-flown to prove it was airworthy." WASPs helped do that. This was an extraordinary time. People were willing to take risks because they believed strongly in the need to win the war.

The women who did these risky jobs graduated mainly from the later classes to enter Jackie Cochran's training program. Women from the first few classes had become

ferry pilots and delivered planes. Jackie found other jobs for her later graduates because she didn't want women to do just one kind of flying. Also, some Army officials didn't want women from the later classes to deliver planes, because they often had less flying experience before joining the WASPs than women from earlier classes. More than half the WASPs never delivered planes. Instead, they tackled the challenging new assignments Jackie found. They handled these difficult missions extremely well, often doing better than some of the male pilots who were assigned to do the same kinds of flying.

TARGET PRACTICE

Jackie began rounding up these extra jobs in the summer of 1943. She started with one of the Army's main flying missions in the United States: the training of anti-aircraft troops (soldiers who shoot down enemy planes). Jackie picked 25 women and sent them to the Army's largest anti-aircraft training center at Camp Davis, on the North Carolina coast. About 600 male pilots were already there, training young anti-aircraft gunners. Many of these pilots didn't like this job; either they had just come back from war and were tired of gunfire or they were newcomers eager to go overseas and fly in real battles. WASPs, however, found this job exciting and did it very well. Soon about 300 WASPs were training anti-aircraft troops at other bases.

To give soldiers sky-high moving targets to aim at, WASPs flew old planes back and forth for hours over the beach near Camp Davis or out in the desert near bases in Texas, New Mexico, and California. "An enlisted guy sat in the back of the plane. He was always scared stiff. He would let a canvas sleeve out from the back of the airplane," recalls Nonie Horton Anderson. A strong metal wire attached this cloth target to the plane (*see photo on title page*). "The gunners down on the desert floor were supposed to shoot at the sleeve. They used live ammunition," says Nonie. Lois Hollingsworth Ziler explains, "Every fourth or fifth bullet was a tracer. It fizzled just like a firecracker so the people that are shooting can see where their bullets are going." WASPs

looking out their cockpit windows could see the puffs of smoke from those exploding bullets. Some planes were hit by mistake, but the damage usually wasn't severe.

Nonie had more fun with the second part of her target-towing missions. After dropping her canvas target down onto the sand, she got to do some buzzing, flying fast and low right over the ground. Buzzing is a stunt that daredevil pilots sometimes do, but it's usually forbidden. In this case, buzzing was OK because it gave soldiers on the ground experience with strafing. That's when a plane, with guns blazing, zooms down over the ground. WASPs didn't fire any guns, but by flying fast right over the soldiers, WASPs let the troops get used to the terror of a strafing attack. Sometimes, WASPs sprayed tear gas to give troops practice snapping on gas masks. Nonie says she flew so fast that "the guy in the back of the plane would be hiding his head."

Most WASPs flew target and strafing missions in single-engine dive-bombers, such as the A-25 Helldiver or the A-24 Douglas Dauntless. Some used bigger planes, including the B-26 Marauder. This big bomber was also used for pretend "dogfighting" (plane-to-plane combat) in which a WASP zoomed through a squad of planes with male crews who aimed at the target fluttering from the WASP's B-26. Some troops "shot" with cameras. They could tell how many "hits" they made by how many pictures they had of the target.

REMOTE CONTROL

A few women used a new invention—remote-control planes—to train troops. Lois and several other WASPs learned to do this at a base in Georgia. Two WASPs flew in a "mother" plane and used a "beep" box to control the target plane—the "baby"—which flew in front of the mother. The baby was a full-size plane but had no pilot in it for these missions. Gunners on the ground shot up toward the baby, trying not to actually hit it. Today, remote-control planes are used to train anti-aircraft troops; pilots no longer have to tow targets.

Other missions were less exciting. "The guys on the ground had to learn how to spot an airplane, track it, figure its speed, that sort of thing," recalls Lois. "So there were some missions when we'd just fly back and forth for a couple of hours." They did this in regular planes, not remote-control ones. Troops on the ground used radar to keep track of the plane. At night, troops used searchlights. WASPs tried not to look into the searchlights, which could blind them for a few minutes so they couldn't see their controls.

DORA DOUGHERTY STROTHER CHECKS THE ENGINE BEFORE A TOW-TARGET MISSION AT CAMP DAVIS.

"WE REALIZED THAT WHAT WE WERE DOING WAS IMPORTANT, SO THE TROOPS COULD LEARN TO FIRE THEIR GUNS ACCURATELY," SAYS DORA, SHOWN HERE CLIMBING OUT OF AN A-25 HELLDIVER.

TROUBLING QUESTIONS

Many of the planes used for towing targets had been in combat and were battered. "The aircraft were often in horrible condition," reports B.J. Mechanics sometimes couldn't fix the planes because spare parts were sent overseas for planes being used in the war. As a result, engines sometimes stalled, causing WASPs to make emergency landings. A few weeks after WASPs arrived at Camp Davis, Mabel Rawlinson's A-24 stalled, crashed, and burst into flames. Mabel wasn't able to escape. She couldn't open the cockpit's roof because the latch didn't work right. She died before help arrived. The plane's repair record noted that the latch needed fixing but hadn't been repaired.

Jackie rushed to Camp Davis to check out the planes WASPs used. She found that although the planes needed repairs, they could be flown safely. Several weeks later, another WASP died in a crash there. Jackie feared that someone had tried to sabotage the plane. Nobody ever discovered what caused that crash. Jackie didn't want an investigation because a scandal—even one that wasn't a WASP's fault—might end the program.

Two WASPs decided to leave, but the rest kept flying. Like all good pilots, WASPs had always inspected their planes thoroughly before takeoff; now they did this even more carefully.

CHECKING WRECKS

Another risky job that Jackie rounded up for her pilots involved test-flying damaged aircraft. "If a fellow crash-landed, the aircraft would be brought back into the base and go in for repair," explains B.J. "When the plane was repaired, before it could go back on the flight line, it had to be tested to make sure it was airworthy. Or if they put a new engine in a plane, we would take it up and 'slow-time' it," by flying at a very slow speed for an hour or so, to break in the new engine.

According to B.J., "Many of the guys didn't like to do this." They'd rather risk their necks in a real air battle overseas instead of by testing a fixed-up plane. WASPs gradually took over most of this testing of repaired planes. "Cadets were forever dinging wing tips or wiping out a landing gear," recalls Gene Shaffer Fitzpatrick.

After a plane was repaired, "they'd have us take it up to see if you can get that wing to fall off." Gene figured "they had us do this because they needed the fellows to be safe to go over and fight the war. We were told that we were expendable. Of course, we always had a parachute and we were supposed to figure out how to get out in time."

WASPs also flew other kinds of missions. Some flew bombers over desert areas so soldiers riding in the planes could learn to drop bombs. Maggie Gee coached men in how to fly using instruments only. Some WASPs helped soldiers learn to fly gliders, which they would use to coast in silently behind enemy lines. Faith Buchner Richards started out ferrying planes but ended up ferrying people. She was one of several WASPs who provided an airborne taxi service for Army officials.

B.J. WILLIAMS

SCARY SPIN

CLOSE-UP

"I had a close call testing an AT-6 that had been in the repair shop many times. They could not figure out what was wrong with it," explains B.J. Williams. "It was ready for testing. None of the fellows would fly it." B.J. gave it a try.

"When you do a test, there's a routine you have to follow. I got it up to 10,000 feet and checked it out on stalls on the way up. It was sluggish. I put it into a spin to see how it recovered, but as I tried to start the recovery, the airplane just kept right on spinning and increasing in speed." It began to spiral down toward the ground.

"They say if you feel death is near, your life will pass in front of you. I suddenly remembered being four years old, sitting on my back porch with colored lollipops." Luckily, she snapped out of her daydream and recalled a tip an instructor gave about what to do if an AT-6 won't stop a spin: Move the control stick in a circle, as if you're whipping mashed potatoes. She grabbed the stick with both hands and pushed it in a circle with all her might. "The airplane wobbled. My heart took a big leap because I thought, 'Now it's responding.'" She got it out of that spin and leveled the plane out at about 500 feet above the ground. Later, she landed and talked with the ground crew, who finally figured out what the plane needed: new wings. B.J. needed a rest.

BREAK TIME

Unlike ferry pilots who were always flying around the country, WASPs who towed targets and tested repaired planes spent most of their time at their home bases. They had more time to enjoy the base's swimming pool, barbecues, dances, and movies. Some even had pet dogs and cats. Dating was easier to arrange. "At Camp Davis there were 40,000 men and few women," reports Dora Dougherty Strother. "We kept a list by the phone in our barracks of whom to date and not to date." Nice guys went on the "to date" list; obnoxious ones made the "not to date" list. Dora adds, "Jackie wanted us to act like ladies, and that's what we did, most of us."

WINNING THEM OVER

WASPS worked at about 120 Army air bases around the country. Most commanders were glad to have these hard-working, dedicated women on their team. But a few commanders didn't like the idea of women flying. Gradually WASPs won them over by doing such a terrific job. Sometimes Jackie had to help, as she did when the Camp Davis commander refused at first to let WASPs fly any target missions. After Jackie did some tough talking, he changed his mind.

Often WASPs worked out problems with their commanders on their own. At B.J.'s base, there were only two WASPs assigned as test pilots. At first their commander wouldn't let them fly at all. So B.J. and the other woman sat quietly outside his office, reading aircraft manuals until the commander's assistant persuaded his boss to let them fly an AT-6. "We flew and won him over," explains B.J. "After that we had no trouble. We always did more than was ever expected of us."

Pitching In

"Just about everyone did something for the war," notes Barbara Erickson London. In addition to the 1,102 WASPs, about 350,000 other women joined women's units that started being set up in 1942 for all branches of the armed forces. Back during World War I, thousands of women served in women's units, but those units closed when that war ended in 1918. For more than 20 years after that, no women, except nurses, could be in the military—until the new units started opening in 1942. Women in these new units couldn't be in combat during World War II, but they did other important jobs. For example, many mechanics who took care of WASP planes were in the WACs (Women's Army Corps). Women in the Navy and the Marines also helped with planes, not as pilots, but as mechanics, air-traffic controllers, flight instructors, and

A WOMAN AIRCRAFT WORKER

navigators. Thousands of women who didn't join the military helped by doing something few women had done before: They worked in factories, replacing men who had to go fight. Women played a big role in aircraft factories, making many of the planes WASPs flew.

Of course, millions of men served in the war. All men age 18 and up had to be in the armed forces, unless excused for health or family reasons, or for doing a war-related job. The Army grew 40 times bigger during the war. Altogether, about 15 million men served in the armed forces.

*WASP PILOTS WITH ONE OF
THE B-17 FLYING FORTRESS BOMBERS THEY FLEW*

THE BIGGIES

WASPs flew every kind of plane the Army had in World War II, including its tough-to-fly biggies: the twin-engine B-26 Marauder and the four-engine bombers—the B-17 Flying Fortress and the B-29 Superfortress, one of the largest planes at the time.

WOMEN TO THE RESCUE

The mighty engines on these aircraft made them more than 20 times as powerful as the open-cockpit PT-19 that pilots used in training. All that power allowed these bombers to fly more than twice as fast as a PT-19. But these bombers and some of the Army's other new planes had a poor reputation for being accident-prone. As a result, some pilots were not eager to fly these big planes.

The Army believed its planes were safe and asked WASPs to prove it. Starting in the fall of 1943, the Army had WASPs learn to fly some of its troublesome planes. Jackie Cochran wrote in her book *The Stars at Noon*, "The obvious conclusion was if a woman could do it, so could a man."

WASPS IN FRONT OF A B-24 LIBERATOR, ANOTHER BIG BOMBER THEY FLEW

MASTERING THE MARAUDER

The twin-engine B-26 Marauder had been in so many accidents that pilots called it the "Widow Maker." At first, this bomber's wings were too short for the heavy weight of the plane and its two powerful engines. Even after the wings were fixed, some pilots were afraid to fly it.

Jackie tried flying a B-26 and decided that if pilots stopped being afraid, they could handle it. She persuaded the Army to try an experiment: Take some WASPs who had never heard bad rumors about the B-26 and teach them to fly it. She picked WASPs who had just graduated from her training program and hadn't been on a regular Army base or heard any B-26 gossip. She sent them to a base in Kansas to take a nine-week course on the B-26.

After completing the course, some of the WASPs flew B-26s as male pilots watched. Jackie noted in her autobiography that the WASPs "made the male pilots' faces red for a while and then the B-26 suddenly became accepted as a safe plane." Men weren't afraid of it anymore. Eventually more than a hundred WASPs mastered the B-26 and used it in target-towing missions.

CONQUERING THE COBRA

The P-39 Aircobra fighter plane also had a deadly nickname: "Flying Coffin." It tended to catch on fire. Its engine was located behind the pilot's seat, not in front as with other fighter planes. Pilots had to handle the P-39 differently. The head of ferrying for the Army, William Tunner (who was now a general) thought his men had trouble with the P-39 because they hadn't taken time to learn about it. He was impressed with women ferry pilots and thought they might make better students. He had five of them learn how to fly the P-39. They discovered they had to use special techniques for takeoff and landing. After mastering those techniques, they flew the plane without any trouble. As word of their success spread, General Tunner reported having "no more complaints from the men."

The women began to deliver P-39s, often taking them to an air base in Montana. From there, men flew the planes to Alaska to give them to Soviet pilots to use in the Soviet Union's battles against the Nazis.

Sometimes, Soviet pilots picked up the planes in Montana. Often the Soviet pilots who flew the planes home were women, members of one of the Soviet Union's women's pilot squadrons. These Russian women not only delivered planes but also flew in combat. Some were nicknamed "Night Witches," because of their nighttime bombing raids. Forty-five years after the war, in 1990, Faith Buchner Richards and Marjorie Osborne Nicol were among about 50 WASPs who went to the Soviet Union to meet some of these daring Night Witches.

A WASP B-26 PILOT

NANCY LOVE
(NEAR RIGHT) AND
BETTY GILLIES

FLYING THE FORTRESS

The Army also asked women to help with one of its big bombers, the B-17 Flying Fortress. Its four engines made it more powerful than the twin-engine B-26. The Army used B-17s a lot, and quite a few had been shot down by enemy troops. By the second half of 1943, many new B-17s were ready to go overseas. But some men ferry pilots felt nervous about flying such a big plane across the Atlantic, especially as stormy winter weather drew near.

General Tunner asked Nancy Love and Betty Gillies to calm the men's worries by flying one of these monsters over the Atlantic to Scotland. Nancy and Betty spent several weeks mastering the B-17 and then delivering three B-17s to bases in the United States. By September 1943, they were ready for their big trip to Scotland to deliver a B-17 named the "Queen Bee" in their honor. They started in Ohio, with a layover in New York, and then made stops in Maine and Labrador.

As they were about to take off from Labrador, General Hap Arnold, head of the Army Air Forces, sent an emer-

gency radio message to the airport to stop the flight. He had been away and had just heard about the trip. All through the war, he never let women fly into a war zone; he wasn't about to change his mind. Nancy and Betty were very disappointed, but they had proved something very important—that women could definitely handle four-engine planes.

Soon more women flew the Flying Fortress. That fall, Jackie sent 17 of her recent graduates to a training base in Ohio to take the Army's three-month B-17 course. This plane was tough to fly. Because it was so heavy, pilots needed a lot a muscle power to operate its foot and hand controls. Thirteen women completed the course. A few stayed at the base in Ohio to test-fly repaired B-17s. The rest went to another base to fly B-17s while young soldiers on board practiced firing the planes' guns.

WASPS WHO TOOK THE B-17 FLYING FORTRESS BOMBER COURSE

ANN BAUMGARTNER CARL

JET PILOT

CLOSE-UP

Ann Baumgartner Carl flew a "biggie" that wasn't huge. Its greatness came from the power of a new kind of engine that was just being developed: the jet engine. All other planes back then had propellers, but not the new plane Ann flew. Jets don't need them. Ann was the first American woman to pilot a jet plane.

Before zooming in a jet, Ann towed targets at Camp Davis. In early 1944, she was sent to Wright Field in Ohio, a special center for testing experimental planes. She and another WASP had to try out new flight suits for women. When this test ended, Ann persuaded officials to let her stay. She became one of Wright Field's expert test pilots, trying out planes and new equipment. She also had a chance to meet the man for whom Wright Field was named—Orville Wright, one of the inventors of the airplane.

Her biggest thrill came on the day she flew the new YP-59A jet. It was top secret and had fake propellers stuck on the front while it sat on the airfield so visitors (and spies) wouldn't find out about it. This jet was never used in battle, but it marked the start of a new era in aviation.

THE B-29 (BELOW) WAS ONE OF WORLD WAR II'S BIGGEST PLANES. TODAY'S JUMBO JETS, SUCH AS A BOEING 747, ARE MUCH MORE POWERFUL. A 747 IS ABOUT TWICE AS LONG AS A B-29.

SHOW-AND-TELL

Two WASPs also tamed the Army's biggest bomber, the B-29 Superfortress, which was almost twice as powerful as the B-17. The B-29 could fly farther than other bombers without having to stop for fuel. The Army needed this new plane badly and rushed it into action without completely solving one of its problems: If it was not flown right, its engines could overheat and catch on fire.

The officer in charge of preparing pilots to fly the B-29—Lieutenant Colonel Paul Tibbets, Jr.—found two WASP tow-target pilots eager to take on this monster: Dora Dougherty Strother and Dorothea Johnson Moorman. In May 1944, he brought them to a base in Alabama and taught them to fly the B-29 in just three days.

Neither woman had ever flown a four-engine plane. Dora thought she might not be big enough to handle it. But she and Dorothea flew the B-29 well. During a training flight, an engine caught on fire, but they handled the emergency and landed safely.

Lieutenant Colonel Tibbets had a picture of Fifi and the name "Ladybird" put on a B-29. Dora and Dorothea flew it to a bomber base in New Mexico to do "show-and-tell" demonstrations. They gave rides to men training to fly the B-29. As the women flew the plane, they explained to their male passengers how to fly it safely. Dora reports that the men discovered that this aircraft wasn't really such a "beast." However, an Army official soon stopped these flights because, as he said, the women were "putting the big football players to shame." Dora and Dorothea went back to other WASP duties and never flew a B-29 again.

"We realized why they had us fly it—showing how easy it was to fly that even a girl could do it. We didn't feel bad about that," explains Dora. "We thought it was a great opportunity for us. We wanted to be part of the effort of proving this plane in any way we could. The whole country was pulling together to win the war."

The men who went on these show-and-tell flights with Dora and Dorothea soon would fly real B-29 bombing missions. Lieutenant Colonel Tibbets flew an important mission the next year. In August 1945, he was the pilot of the B-29 that dropped an atomic bomb on Hiroshima, an attack that was devastating and tragic for that Japanese city and its people, but which helped bring this long, brutal war to an end.

DOROTHEA JOHNSON MOORMAN (ABOVE, LEFT) AND
DORA DOUGHERTY STROTHER WITH LIEUTENANT COLONEL
PAUL TIBBETS, JR. IN FRONT OF THE "LADYBIRD" B-29
SUPERFORTRESS BOMBER

JACKIE COCHRAN REVIEWING HER TOW-TARGET PILOTS

10

SENT HOME
TOO SOON

"They taught us how to fly, now they send us home to cry, 'cause they don't want us anymore." Those are the words from a song WASPs made up because of a letter every WASP received in early October 1944. It came from the leader of the Army Air Forces, General Hap Arnold. The letter gave WASPs the sad news that their program would end on December 20, 1944. "We felt so bad," recalls Dora Dougherty Strother. "We enjoyed what we were doing. We felt we were contributing. We felt needed." She and other WASPs had done an amazing job. So why, as Bernice Falk Haydu asked, were they "kicking us out"?

HIGH HOPES

In early 1944, months before General Arnold's letter arrived, WASPs had high hopes. "I think that we all expected to get into the military," explains Faith Buchner Richards. After all, Congress had started considering a bill in February 1944 that would finally make WASPs part of the Army Air Forces. WASPs started looking more like military pilots that spring when their new Santiago blue uniforms arrived. About 400 WASPs began learning how to be Army officers by taking the Army's four-week officer-training course.

A few WASPs didn't want to be part of the Army. They wanted to be able to resign at any time, something that's not easy to do in the Army. But most WASPs looked forward to becoming officers in the Army Air Forces. They'd be paid as much as male pilots and be covered by the Army's insurance. More important, they'd feel accepted as full members of the team.

FOOT-SOLDIER FEARS

Unfortunately, the WASP bill reached Congress right after the Army made a group of men so angry that they set out to destroy the WASPs. These men were flight instructors in the Army's pilot training schools for men, which had been turning out a steady stream of new pilots for the war. In January 1944, the Army said it would close these schools soon because they had trained all the new pilots the Army could use. One reason the Army didn't need more new pilots was that, thankfully, not as many pilots had been killed in battle as had been feared. Also, the WASPs had done such a great job of taking over noncombat flying that more of the male pilots the Army already had could go overseas into battle.

The United States was getting ready to invade Nazi-controlled Europe in a few months—the big D-day invasion—and possibly later to invade Japan as well. Although the Army had enough pilots for these invasions, it didn't have enough infantry troops (foot soldiers who fight on the ground). Instead of encouraging young men to become pilots, it wanted to sign them up for the infantry.

The thousands of flight instructors—or men learning to be instructors—were civilians. They had been excused from joining the Army as long as they trained pilots. If their schools closed, the instructors could be drafted

and might end up as foot soldiers. To keep that from happening, they tried to take over the WASPs' jobs. But many of these men weren't very experienced. They had taught beginning flying and would need a lot of training to handle the advanced planes WASPs flew.

The Army promised to treat the instructors fairly. It would let them try out to be Army pilots; if they didn't make it, they could do other flying-related jobs in the Army. But those promises didn't calm the men's fears. They organized a huge publicity campaign to persuade Congress to defeat the bill that would make WASPs part of the Army Air Forces. The men and their supporters sent hundreds of letters to Congress. Articles in newspapers and magazines claimed it wasn't fair for women to be military pilots if men wanted those jobs.

Many articles said things that were not true, such as that WASPs weren't good pilots and had more accidents than men. Articles also claimed it cost more to train WASPs than men and that WASP uniforms cost more. In each case, the opposite was true. WASPs flew well and had a lower accident rate than men flying the same missions. It cost the same to train a WASP as to train a male pilot, and WASP uniforms cost the government less than uniforms for male officers.

WOMEN FACTORY WORKERS WHO PUT RIVETS ON AIRCRAFT IN WORLD WAR II EARNED THE NICKNAME "ROSIE THE RIVETER."

Pioneers

WASPs weren't the only women criticized back then for doing a so-called man's job. People felt it was OK for women to help in an emergency, and at the start of the war, articles praised women for working in factories or joining the WACs. But in 1944, as the war seemed about to end, many people felt women should go back to being homemakers. After the war, it was hard for women to find jobs that used the skills they learned in their wartime jobs. However, these pioneers had shown what women could do and helped set the stage for the women's movement of the 1960s and 1970s.

Hollywood Didn't Help

As Congress considered the WASP bill, a new movie opened: *Ladies Courageous.* It was about the WASPs, but the characters in the movie were more interested in flirting and gossiping than in being pilots. "It was horrible," Caro Bayley Bosca decided when she saw the movie at a theater near her base. "I was never so embarrassed in my life . . . everybody here knew it was rotten and sympathized with us." However, everybody in Congress may not have known that. This movie may have helped turn some congressmen against the WASPs.

A WASP READS ABOUT THE JUNE 6, 1944, D-DAY INVASION.

GROUNDED

General Arnold was one of the few people who spoke up for the WASPs. He testified before Congress, where he spoke about the WASPs' excellent performance record. Representative John Costello of California, who wrote the WASP bill, told Congress that he did not think a woman should be discriminated against.

A few congressional representatives agreed, but not enough. On June 21, 1944, Congress defeated the WASP bill. This vote came just a few weeks after the successful June 6 D-day invasion of Europe.

This vote didn't end the WASPs. They could have kept on working for the military without actually being in it. Some people also suggested that WASPs could join the WACs—the women's group of the Army—but Jackie Cochran didn't like that. WAC commanders weren't pilots. Jackie felt they wouldn't know how to deal with pilots. She sent a report to General Arnold that listed the WASPs' many achievements and made an all-or-nothing demand: If WASPs couldn't be in the Army Air Forces, like all other Army pilots, the WASP program should end. Her gamble failed. General Arnold was too busy directing the air war over Europe to work on a new WASP bill. So he sent every WASP a letter announcing the end of the WASP program. His letter said:

"I am very proud of you young women. . . . When we needed you, you came through and have served most commendably under very difficult circumstances. . . . You have freed male pilots for other work, but now the war situation has changed and the time has come when your volunteered services are no longer needed. . . . My sincerest thanks and Happy Landings always."

A FAREWELL PARTY FOR
BARBARA ERICKSON LONDON
(CUTTING THE CAKE)
AND OTHER FERRY PILOTS
AT THEIR BASE IN
LONG BEACH, CALIFORNIA

WHAT A BLOW

"It was very disappointing, terribly hard. We knew we were badly needed," recalls Barbara Erickson London. "The Ferry Command tried very hard to get the ferry group to stay. We volunteered to do it for free, or for a dollar a year." Several commanders asked if their WASPs could stay. But the Army turned them all down.

"So we just had to go home," explains Barbara, who recalls that the morning she left her base in California to go home, "there were 51 aircraft sitting on the runway that didn't get delivered that day." Faith notes, "The war was still going on . . . that was the thing that hurt. We couldn't contribute."

Many WASPs wanted to keep flying and wrote to the airlines to find jobs as pilots. "I was as qualified as some of the guys," recalls Barbara. "But the airlines just sent me back an application for being a stewardess." Airlines still wouldn't hire women as pilots.

Some WASPs found jobs teaching flying or selling aircraft, but they never again did the kind of flying they loved as WASPs. It was especially tough for people like Marjorie Osborne Nicol, whose class graduated in November 1944 and had only a month of active duty.

It was hard on Jackie, too. At Marjorie's graduation, Jackie stood up to give a speech, "but tears started rolling down her cheeks and she was forced to sit down," a friend of Marjorie's reported. At the last graduation ceremony in December, Jackie held back her tears to tell her WASPs how proud she was of them, noting, "My greatest accomplishment in aviation has been the small part I have played in helping make possible the results you have shown."

Some base commanders gave WASPs going-away parties and found them flights home. At other bases, WASPs just packed up and left. "We felt lost," recalls B.J. Williams, "like fish out of water."

Flight Note

HIGH PRAISE: Here's what General Hap Arnold, commander of the Army Air Forces, said at the last WASP graduation on December 7, 1944:

"Frankly, I didn't know in 1941 whether a slip of a young girl could fight the controls of a B-17. . . . Well, now in 1944 . . . we can come to only one conclusion—the entire operation has been a success. It is on the record that women can fly as well as men. . . . You have worked hard. . . . you have buckled down to the monotonous, the routine jobs which are not much desired by our hot-shot young men headed toward combat. . . . In some of your jobs I think they [commanders] like you better than men. . . . Every WASP . . . has filled a vital and necessary place in the jigsaw pattern of victory."

SCORECARD

25,000	women applied to join the women's pilot program.
1,830	women were accepted into Jackie's training program.
1,102	women served as WASPs (1,074 graduates from Jackie's training program + the 28 WAFS "Originals").
38	women pilots died serving their country.
12,652	planes were delivered by women ferry pilots.
77	kinds of planes were flown by women ferry pilots.
60,000,000	miles were flown by WASPs.

WHAT A RECORD

"The WASPs . . . leave behind them a truly impressive and unprecedented record, one with which I am sincerely proud to have been associated," wrote General William Tunner, who had been in charge of the Army's plane-delivery units. Words of praise like this came from other commanders as well. They realized what an important job the WASPs had done. After the war, the Army honored the two WASP leaders, giving Nancy Love an Air Medal and awarding Jackie Cochran the Distinguished Service Medal.

WASPs had helped make possible victory in the war by delivering warplanes, training troops, testing aircraft, and taking over other noncombat flying. In just two years, WASPs piloted every kind of plane the Army had, flying a total of 60 million miles. That's like flying around the Earth almost 2,500 times.

The WASP record proved that "the physical endurance of WASPs is basically equal to that of male pilots," as Jackie wrote in her final report. At first, some commanders had worried about this and had tried to ground women during their menstrual periods. Nancy stopped that. In addition, Jackie had the doctor at the WASP training center keep careful records, including having women report when they had their periods. The doctor found that WASPs flew as well at that time of the month as at any other. WASPs lost less flying time for being sick than men doing the same jobs.

Army commanders also admired the women's spirit. "It is a quality which . . . cannot be measured merely in the number of hours flown," said Lieutenant General Barton Yount. "It is the quality of courage—of courage in the face of danger."

MAGGIE GEE

SHY NO MORE

"I was sorry it was over," recalls Maggie Gee. "It was a big disappointment, but you have to face reality. You could hang around and feel sorry for yourself. If you have something to go back to, that makes a big difference. I had one year of college before the war. I went back to school."

The WASPs gave her a lot of self-confidence. "Before, I was just a shy girl. When I went back to college, I became president of the Chinese Association. I got involved in things." After finishing at the University of California in Berkeley, she worked in a physics research laboratory. "I didn't keep up with flying. I didn't have any money. I was too busy going to school and earning a living," she notes.

"For the short period of time I was in the WASPs I made a lot of friends. Here it is, years later, and we're all still good friends."

BOUNCING BACK

A few WASPs had trouble dealing with their disappointment, but most bounced back, partly because, as Barbara notes, flying Army planes "gave you a tremendous amount of confidence."

"Any time somebody shuts the door on you like that, and if you feel you did nothing wrong, just take it on the chin," advises Florene Miller Watson. "Pick yourself up and get on with something else. I went back to college." So did Dora, but it took her ten years to finish; she took classes part-time because she had to earn money for college bills. She worked as a flight instructor while earning a college degree from Northwestern University and a master's degree from the University of Illinois. The government didn't give WASPs money for college as it did to "official" veterans (people who served in the military) because WASPs weren't officially in the military.

"I went home and cried for a while," recalls Gene Shaffer Fitzpatrick. She didn't keep flying. She couldn't afford to buy a plane or rent one. She found a job in an office. Soon she married and had kids, like many WASPs and other women in the 1950s. When her kids were teenagers, she finally started flying again and became a flight instructor, as did many WASPs. Margaret Ray Ringenberg became a flight instructor and then started entering air races when she was in her 30s. In 1994, at age 72, she flew in an around-the-world air race.

WATCH OUT!

For many years, most of the women didn't talk much about being WASPs. "If you told people you flew military planes, they looked at you as if you were crazy," recalls Faith. Newspapers, magazines, and even the military seemed to forget about the WASPs. When the war ended in August 1945—almost eight months after WASPs went home—newspapers didn't tell how the women pilots had helped. Nonie observes, "We were the best-kept secret of the war." But about 30 years after the war, something happened that made WASPs speak up.

Some women found other ways to keep up with flying. Barbara and her pilot husband opened an aircraft sales business. Betty Gillies helped run the Powder Puff Derby, a women's air race that several WASPs flew in for many years. After college, Dora worked as an engineer at an aircraft company, designing things like helicopter cockpits. A few WASPs worked for airlines, but not as pilots. Faith helped run an airline reservations department. Nonie Horton Anderson was a technical writer for several airlines. B.J. worked for two aircraft manufacturers, writing and producing films and videos about the companies' planes and missiles.

Some women switched to other careers. Florene taught business at a college. Maggie worked as a physicist in a research laboratory. Teresa James helped run her family's florist shop. Other WASPs became judges, doctors, nurses, writers, lawyers, artists, teachers, photographers—even actresses. Nancy became a mom, a flying one with her own plane. Jackie ran her cosmetics business and kept setting flying records.

In 1947, the Air Force was created as a separate branch of the armed forces. Teresa joined the Air Force Reserves as an officer. So did many WASPs, including Nonie, Dora, Barbara, and B.J. They couldn't be pilots because the Air Force still wouldn't let women fly, but they did other important duties in the Reserves while holding down regular jobs. For example, B.J. wrote and produced Air Force films.

WASPS PROUDLY CARRYING THE FLAG AT AVENGER FIELD

AN AIR FORCE CADET
STANDS BY A STATUE THAT
HONORS THE WASPS
AT THE AIR FORCE ACADEMY
IN COLORADO SPRINGS,
COLORADO.

11

UP, UP, AND AWAY

About 30 years after the WASP program ended, women pilots finally had a chance to fly for the U.S. military again. The Navy came first, letting eight young women into pilot training in 1973. Next came the Army. Then, in 1976, the Air Force signed up a small group of women for pilot training. It was too late for the WASPs, but they were happy for the younger women.

However, the WASPs were not happy when news reports claimed that the new pilots were the first women to fly U.S. military aircraft. No way! WASPs flew military planes before the new women pilots were even born. Elaine Danforth Harmon reports that WASPs "heard a newscaster say that this would be the first time women would fly military aircraft. Boy! That's what got us together!"

RIGHTING A WRONG

Over the years, many WASPs had lost track of one another. B.J. Williams and others had started a WASP organization. It kept a list of where they all were and sponsored reunions and other activities. Teresa James and several others kept trying to persuade the government to state that the women had really been military pilots. Nothing came of her efforts until those news reports fired up the WASPs to speak out.

This time they had friends in Congress, including Senator Barry Goldwater, who was the Republican candidate for President in 1964. He had been a ferry pilot during the war and thought WASPs were terrific. He was one of the sponsors of a new bill that said WASPs should be considered to have served in the military and should be treated like all other veterans.

To make sure this bill would pass, WASPs did what their opponents did in 1944: They organized a huge publicity campaign. They declared 1977 The Year of the WASP. WASP volunteers set up an office in Washington, D.C. They wrote fact sheets and met with congressional representatives. Around the country, WASPs collected signatures on petitions asking Congress to pass the WASP bill. They talked reporters into writing stories in favor of the WASPs. B.J. created a short Air Force film about the WASPs that ran on TV news shows.

Some veterans' groups tried to stop the WASP bill, but they were no match for WASPs like Dora Dougherty Strother, who by then was an important aircraft company official. She spoke to the committee in Congress that was considering the bill and explained that the millions of miles WASPs flew had indeed been for military missions.

By 1977, attitudes toward women had changed. The women's movement of the 1960s created a feeling that women should have the same opportunities as men. There wasn't a military draft anymore. People didn't have to join the military. They joined only if they wanted to serve. To encourage young women to sign up, it would help to end the unfair treatment of WASPs.

The WASP bill passed. On November 23, 1977, President Jimmy Carter signed it into law, making it official that WASPs had served on "active duty in the Armed Forces of the United States." Nancy Love had died of cancer the year before, but Jackie Cochran was able to see her WASPs receive this well-deserved honor. About a year and a half later, the Air Force started giving WASPs what is given to all veterans who serve their country well: honorable discharges.

More honors followed. Many of the women have received awards from aviation organizations and other groups. Exhibits about the WASPs have appeared in many museums, including the National Air and Space Museum, in Washington, D.C.

DORA DOUGHERTY STROTHER (FAR LEFT) WITH OTHER WASPS WHO WORKED WITH SENATOR BARRY GOLDWATER (SEATED) TO GET THE 1977 WASP BILL PASSED

OPENING THE SKIES

"Without the WASPs we wouldn't be here," says Kimberly Olson, one of the new young women pilots of the 1970s. She was in one of the first classes to complete Air Force pilot training, graduating in 1979. Now she is an Air Force colonel. "When we started, men in the Air Force still worried whether women could handle the stress of flying." She feels the WASP record "gave us the historical data we needed to prove that women could fly and be very successful."

That made things a little easier for the new pilots. But they still had to prove themselves, to convince officials that women could handle all kinds of missions, including flying in combat, which women finally received permission to do in 1993.

WASPs are proud of the new women pilots and even sent the first Air Force recruits Fifi stickers for their helmets. The new pilots admire the WASPs for paving the way.

TWO OF TODAY'S WOMEN PILOTS: COLONEL KIMBERLY OLSON, UNITED STATES AIR FORCE (NEAR RIGHT) AND M'LIS WARD, A PILOT FOR UNITED AIR LINES

Together WASPs and the new pilots started an organization called Women Military Aviators to encourage other women to fly. In the year 2000, more than 600 women served as pilots in all branches of the armed forces; hundreds more were navigators. The military doesn't have separate units for women anymore. Women now serve along with men.

Not only military pilots are grateful for the WASPs' pioneering efforts. In 1973, airlines finally started hiring women pilots. One of the first was Terry London Rinehart, daughter of Barbara Erickson London. In 1976, when Terry was hired, only about 10 women worked as airline pilots; now there are 4,000 worldwide, with most in the United States.

FLY ON

A bronze statue of a young woman gazing up toward the sky stands at the Air Force Academy in Colorado Springs, Colorado. She's a WASP, with Fifi on her flight suit. She stands near a statue that honors other pioneering pilots of World War II, the African-American Tuskegee airmen. Dorothy Swain Lewis, a WASP who became an artist, created the WASP statue. It reminds Air Force cadets to keep looking up, to meet new challenges bravely, as WASPs did.

"My mother didn't talk much about being a WASP when I was growing up," recalls Terry, who started flying as a teen. "It wasn't until I got into aviation that I realized what a feat it was to climb into a different aircraft every day and fly it across the country by yourself. Today we wouldn't do that." Pilots today are usually qualified to fly just a few kinds of planes. "It's amazing what these women did, without a lot of fanfare or publicity. They just went out and did it and had a great time. I look at my mother's log book and I look at some of the planes that she flew and I go, 'Wow! That's really incredible!'" Terry feels that learning about the WASPs gave her a sense of "self-confidence and encouragement for women to do things out of the norm."

The story of the WASPs isn't just about flying. It's about doing your best even when things get tough. As a 13-year-old from Long Island said after writing a school report on the WASPs: "It's important to know that people who weren't that much older than us and that lived when women were still looked down upon, could do something so great." WASP B.J. Williams advises, "If you have a dream of something you want to do, and you prepare yourself and stay focused, go for it."

TIPS ON BECOMING A PILOT TODAY

"Flying is less risky today than it was for the WASPs," says NASA astronaut Colonel Eileen Collins. Lieutenant Brigitte Lott, a Navy pilot, agrees, "We have more safety measures built into planes now. Also, if there's ever anything wrong with a plane, it gets fixed immediately." What can kids do who want to become a pilot?

NAVY PILOT
LIEUTENANT
BRIGITTE LOTT

"DO WELL IN SCHOOL, ESPECIALLY IN MATH AND SCIENCE," advises astronaut Collins. Lieutenant Lott agrees, "You don't have to major in math or science in college. I majored in English. But I took math and science, too; they're a good foundation for flying."

"STAY IN SHAPE," adds Colonel Collins. "Eat right, exercise right, stay away from drugs and alcohol. For pilots, it's important to be in good physical condition."

"FIND OUT ABOUT FLYING," says Colonel Collins. She recommends reading books, joining aviation clubs, or working on aviation badges in Scouts. Learn about other aviation careers, such as navigator, air-traffic controller, engineer, flight attendant, or airport manager. She doesn't think kids need to take flying lessons; she didn't take one until she was 20. Air Force pilot Colonel Kimberly Olson feels a trial lesson can help kids discover if flying is for them. However, kids can't solo until age 16 and must be 17 to get a license. For books and Web sites, see the Resource Guide on the next page.

CHRONOLOGY

1939	World War II starts in Europe. The United States isn't in the war yet.
	Jackie Cochran writes to Eleanor Roosevelt, suggesting how women pilots can help.
1940	Nancy Love writes to the Army, suggesting that women pilots could ferry planes.
1941	December 7: Pearl Harbor is attacked by Japanese planes. The United States enters World War II.
1942	Two programs for women pilots begin: The WAFS, Nancy Love's ferry squadron; and the WFTD, Jackie Cochran's training program.
1943	WAFS and WFTD join to form the WASPs, Women Airforce Service Pilots.
1944	June 6: D-day invasion of Nazi-controlled Europe by the United States and its allies.
	June 21: Congress defeats the WASP bill, preventing WASPs from officially joining the Army Air Forces.
	December 20: the WASP program ends.
1945	World War II ends.
1947	The U.S. Air Force is created as a separate branch of the armed forces.
1973	Airlines start to hire women pilots.
	The Navy and Army let a few women start pilot training.
1976	The Air Force lets women into pilot training.
1977	President Carter signs a bill that declares that the WASPs served on "active duty in the Armed Forces of the United States."

BOOKS ABOUT WASPS

Most books about the WASPs are written for adults, but here are a few that may interest younger readers.

Carl, Ann B. *A WASP Among Eagles*. Smithsonian Institution Press. Washington, DC: 1999.

Cochran, Jacqueline. *The Stars at Noon*. Little Brown. Boston, MA: 1954.

Keil, Sally VanWagenen. *Those Wonderful Women in Their Flying Machines*. Four Directions Press. NY: 1990.

Merryman, Molly. *Clipped Wings*. New York University Press. NY: 1998.

Noggle, Anne. *For God, Country and the Thrill of It*. Texas A & M University Press. College Station, TX: 1990.

Ringenberg, Margaret J. with Jane L. Roth. *Girls Can't Be Pilots*. Daedalus Press. Fort Wayne, IN: 1998.

Roberts, Marjorie H. *Wingtip to Wingtip*. Aviatrix Publishing. Arlington Heights, IL: 2000.

Simbeck, Rob. *Daughter of the Air: The Brief Soaring Life of Cornelia Fort*. Atlantic Monthly Press. NY: 1999.

Verges, Marianne. *On Silver Wings*. Ballantine Books. NY: 1991.

Williams, Vera S. *WASPs*. Motorbooks International. Osceola, WI: 1994.

OTHER BOOKS

Bragg, Janet Harmon. *Soaring Above Setbacks*. Smithsonian Institution Press. Washington, DC: 1996.

Flowers, Sandra H. and Michael H. Abbott. *Women in Aviation and Space*. U.S. Department of Transportation, Federal Aviation Administration. (Can be downloaded from this Web site: www.faa.gov)

McKissack, Patricia and Frederick. *Red-Tail Angels*. Walker. NY: 1995.

Szabo, Corinne. *Sky Pioneer: A Photobiography of Amelia Earhart*. National Geographic Society. Washington, DC: 1997.

WEB SITES

These Web sites have more information on the WASPs or on women in aviation.

www.beapilot.com – Be A Pilot organization

www.pbs.org/wgbh/amex/flygirls/ – The "Fly Girls" section of the PBS Web site

http://spacelink.nasa.gov – NASA headquarters

www.twu.edu/library/collections.htm – Texas Woman's University Library*

www.ninety-nines.org – The Ninety-Nines, the International Organization of Women Pilots

www.wpafb.af.mil/museum/ – United States Air Force Museum

www.wasp-wwii.org – WASP on the Web*

www.wiai.org – Women in Aviation International

www.womensmemorial.org/ – Women in Military Service for America Memorial

Web site that provides a more complete list of WASP books

VIDEOS

Fly Girls. PBS Home Video.

Women of Courage. The Story of the Women Pilots of World War II. K.M. Productions.

ACKNOWLEDGMENTS

I first heard about the WASPs in 1995 and set out to write about them in a book for young people. With help from Texas Woman's University, I interviewed ten of the women by telephone. They were full of energy and enthusiasm and very patient about explaining things, because I'm not a pilot. I'm very grateful to all of them: Nonie Horton Anderson, Gene Shaffer Fitzpatrick, Maggie Gee, Teresa James, Barbara Erickson London, Faith Buchner Richards, Margaret Ray Ringenberg, Dora Dougherty Strother, Florene Miller Watson, and Betty Jane Williams. Most quotes from them in the book come from these interviews. Thanks also to the following, who were kind enough to share with me their views on the WASPs: Col. Eileen Collins; Col. Kimberly Olson; Lt. Marcelyn Atwood, USAF; Lt. Brigitte Lott, U.S. Navy; Terry Rinehart, Delta Airlines; M'Lis Ward, United Airlines; Lucy Young, U.S. Air; Hannah Love Robinson (Nancy Love's daughter); Pete and Glen Gillies (Betty Gillies's son and granddaughter); Rob Simbeck; and WASP enthusiast Jenny Gamell. Quotes from additional WASPs and from other individuals, along with excerpts from WASP songs, come mainly from oral histories, letters, and documents in the Woman's Collection of the Texas Woman's University Library or from the Franklin D. Roosevelt Library in Hyde Park, New York. I read nearly every book written about the WASPs/WAFS. Many are listed in the Resource Guide. As noted below, a few quotes used in my book come from some of these sources. For a more complete list of books, visit: www.WASP-wwii.org or www.twu.edu/library/collections.htm

Many people helped bring this book to life. Special thanks go to Dawn Letson of Texas Woman's University and to Jacquelyn Anderson, Larchmont Library. I'm also grateful to Deborah Douglas, author of *United States Women in Aviation 1940–1985* (Smithsonian Institution Press, 1990), who read the manuscript and gave valuable advice, as did Barbara Erickson London, Betty Jane Williams, and Dora Dougherty Strother. Yvonne Kincaid, Air Force historian, helped pinpoint important facts, as did Ike Kibbe, Piper Aviation Museum, and Donald S. Lopez, National Air and Space Museum. Thanks for help with this project also go to the following Air Force personnel: Lt. Lars Anderson, 2nd Lt. Angela Arredondo, Cadet 1C Kendra Marks, Lt. Col. Sue Laushine, Maj. Michael Shavers, SSgt. Angela Stafford, Dennis Case, Lonna McKinley, Jerry Rep, and Jeffery S. Underwood. I am also grateful to the Navy's Lt. jg. Susan D. Henson, Lt. jg. Andrea Kowal, and Christopher J. Madden. Special thanks for arranging for Col. Eileen Collins's contribution to the book go to NASA's Johnson Space Center and its staff members Lucy Lytwynsky, Doug Peterson, Kelly O. Humphries, and Mike Gentry. Thanks also to Patricia Gillies Astier, Ann McGuffin Barton, Tom Brokaw, Dave Burgevin, Mike Cardell, Nancy Durr, Kate Igoe, Hugh Morgan, Joan Piper, Dom Pisano, Katherine Williams, Kay Woodson, Dr. Jay Zagorsky, my editor, Suzanne Fonda, and, of course, Carl, Eric, and Noah Nathan.

NOTES

Quotes from Cornelia Fort on pages 15 and 49 come from Fort, Cornelia. "At the Twilight's Last Gleaming," *Woman's Home Companion,* June 1943. Her letter on page 58 has appeared in several books including Simbeck, Rob. *Daughter of the Air.* Atlantic Monthly Press. NY: 1999.

Quotes from Jacqueline Cochran on pages 17, 67, and 68 come from Cochran, Jacqueline. *The Stars at Noon.* Little Brown. Boston, MA: 1954.

The quotes from Jacqueline Cochran and Captain Garrett on page 29 appear in Verges, Marianne. *On Silver Wings.* Ballantine Books. NY: 1991; and Moolman, Valerie. *Women Aloft.* Time-Life Books. Arlington, VA: 1981.

The quote from Dora Dougherty Strother on page 21 comes from the PBS video *Fly Girls.*

Quotes from Janet Harmon Bragg on page 27 come from her autobiography, *Soaring Above Setbacks.* Smithsonian Institution Press. Washington, DC: 1996.

The P-51 pilot anecdote on page 55 comes from Granger, Byrd Howell. *On Final Approach.* Falconer Publishing Company. Scottsdale, AZ: 1991.

The quote from General Tunner on page 68 comes from Tunner, William H. *Over the Hump.* Duell, Sloan and Pearce. NY: 1964.

INDEX

Boldface indicates illustrations